D0601060

FamilyCircle

Big Book of Christmas

WITHDRAWN

CONTRA COSTA COUNTY LIBRARY

3 1901 03061 6900

A LEISURE ARTS PUBLICATION

FamilyCircle
Big Book of Christmas

LEISURE ARTS

Vice President and Editor-in-Chief: Anne Van Wagner Childs
Executive Director: Sandra Graham Case
Publications Director: Carla Bentley
Editorial Director: Susan Frantz Wiles
Test Kitchen Director/Foods Editor: Celia Fahr Harkey, R.D.
Design Director: Patricia Wallenfang Sowers
Creative Art Director: Gloria Bearden
Senior Graphics Art Director: Melinda Stout

FAMILY CIRCLE

Editor-in-Chief: Susan Kelliher Ungaro
Executive Editor: Barbara Winkler
Food Director: Peggy Katalinich
Home Editor: Lauren Hunter
How-To's Editor: Kathryn Rubinstein

G+J USA PUBLISHING

Books & Licensing Manager: Tammy Palazzo
Books & Licensing Coordinator: Eileen C. Lamadore

LEISURE ARTS EDITORIAL STAFF

EDITORIAL
Managing Editor: Linda L. Trimble
Editorial Coordinator: Terri Leming Davidson
Associate Editors: Stacey Robertson Marshall and
  Janice Teipen Wojcik

TECHNICAL
Managing Editor: Sherry Taylor O'Connor
Associate Editor: Beth M. Knife
Administrative Coordinator: Debra Nettles
Publications Assistant: Heather Bakalekos

FOODS
Assistant Foods Editor: Jane Kenner Prather
Test Kitchen Home Economist: Rose Glass Klein
Test Kitchen Coordinator: Nora Faye Taylor
Test Kitchen Assistants: Camille T. Alstadt and Melissa Adams

ART
Book/Magazine Graphics Art Director: Diane M. Hugo
Photography Stylists: Beth Carter, Sondra Daniel, Karen Hall,
  Aurora Huston, and Christina Myers

DESIGN
Designers: Sandra Spotts Ritchie, Anne Pulliam Stocks,
  and Linda Diehl Tiano
Executive Assistants: Debra Smith and Billie Steward
Craft Assistant: Melanie Vaughan

PROMOTIONS
Managing Editors: Alan Caudle and Marjorie Ann Lacy
Associate Editors: Debby Carr, Ellen J. Clifton, Steven M. Cooper,
  and Dixie L. Morris
Designer: Dale Rowett
Art Director: Linda Lovette Smart
Publishing Systems Administrator: Cynthia M. Lumpkin
Publishing Systems Assistants: Susan Mary Gray and Robert Walker

LEISURE ARTS BUSINESS STAFF

Publisher: Rick Barton
Vice President and General Manager: Thomas L. Carlisle
Vice President, Finance: Tom Siebenmorgen
Vice President, Marketing: Bob Humphrey
Vice President, National Accounts: Pam Stebbins
Retail Marketing Director: Margaret Sweetin

General Merchandise Manager: Cathy Laird
Vice President, Operations: Brian U. Davis
Distribution Director: Rob Thieme
Retail Customer Service Director: Tonie B. Maulding
Retail Customer Service Managers: Carolyn Pruss and Wanda Price
Print Production Manager: Fred F. Pruss

Copyright© 1998 by Leisure Arts, Inc., 5701 Ranch Drive, Little Rock, Arkansas 72212, and G+J USA Publishing, 375 Lexington Avenue, New York, New York 10017-5514. All rights reserved. No part of this book may be reproduced in any form or by any means without the prior written permission of the publisher, except for brief quotations in reviews appearing in magazines or newspapers. We have made every effort to ensure that these recipes and instructions are accurate and complete. We cannot, however, be responsible for human error, typographical mistakes, or variations in individual work. Printed in the United States of America. First Printing.

Library of Congress Catalog Number 98-66514
Hardcover ISBN: 1-57486-114-X
Softcover ISBN: 1-57486-098-4

10 9 8 7 6 5 4 3 2 1

introduction

Christmas is, indeed, a most wonderful time of the year, and Family Circle brings you the most delightful ways to celebrate it! Inside this Big Book of Christmas, *you'll find our very best creations for decorating, gift-giving, and entertaining. The simple-to-follow instructions will lead you through a whole spectrum of crafting skills so you can enjoy the merriment of a gaily adorned home and beautiful handmade finery. Each section opens with an assortment of at-a-glance ideas for instant frills and festive flavors. You'll discover a variety of designs — from country casual to sophisticated chic — to use all through the house, right up to the tip-top of the tree. We've even included handcrafted presents for everyone on your list, along with sumptuous recipes to share and serve. From our homes to yours, we hope these pages bring you a sleighful of holiday fun, and we wish you all the joy of the Yuletide!*

cont

home for the holidays

6

all the trimmings

30

share the joy

46

ents

festive traditions

eat, drink, and be merry

72

80

home for the holidays

It's easy to fill your whole house with holiday cheer! Stitch up a Nativity wall hanging or a family of snow people, create a stunning needlework pillow, or craft a rustic Santa. Extend the jolly mood to every room with the projects in this chapter, including the quick ideas here!

1.

2.

3.

Make every nook and cranny more inviting with simple accents:
1. Display assorted ornaments in a pedestal bowl. 2. Don't
forget to hang the mistletoe — and add a red checked bow!
3. Wrap fruit with fabric strips; secure with cloves and line
up on a narrow tray or your mantel. 4. Let teddy bears greet
visitors with a vibrant "Noel!" 5. Top frames with bundles of
greenery and trims. 6. Pile flowers, fruit, nuts, and whole spices
in a bowl to make a fragrant centerpiece. 7. For country charm,
tie gingham ribbon to a lampshade. 8. Decorate Kriss Kringle
cookies with colorful icing to delight young and old alike.

get set for christmas

a lustrous table twinkling with glints of gold amid sprigs of greenery is simply beautiful — and simple to do! Centerpiece topiaries (opposite) are swathed with metallic tissue. Mark place settings with rubber-stamped name cards (right) and pomander favors, and use greenery and berries to festoon chairbacks. Fill the china cabinet with a holiday mix: pine boughs, fruit, gold-leafed nuts, foil-wrapped chocolates, and glass decanters of water flavored with oranges and cherries.

9

the christmas story

recall the story of the very first Christmas with handcrafted adornments. An elegant cross-stitched tableau captures the wonder of that long-ago night.

How-To's on pages 106-107

Stained-Glass Ornament

You need: Aleene's Clear Shrink-It™ Plastic; ¾ yd of ³⁄₁₆"W gold cord; iridescent black dimensional-paint writer; gold rub-on metallic finish; tissue paper – cream, dark red, purple, light turquoise, dark turquoise; paintbrushes; decoupage glue; permanent pen; low-temp glue gun.

Outlining design: Use permanent pen to trace black and grey outlines of pattern (page 108) onto plastic. Use dimensional-paint writer to paint over grey lines of pattern on plastic. Let dry.

Applying tissue paper: *All "stained glass" areas (except gold) are colored by gluing tissue paper pieces to unpainted side (back) of plastic. Apply all pieces of one color of tissue paper at a time and let dry before moving to next color.* Place one color of tissue over pattern and draw around each area of that color onto tissue; cut out just outside lines. Apply a thin coat of decoupage glue to corresponding areas on back of plastic; press tissue cutouts into glue. Use paintbrush to apply a coat of glue over tissue cutouts, wrinkling tissue slightly with brush. Repeat for all tissue paper colors.

Applying rub-on finish: For gold areas on pattern, use paintbrush and follow manufacturer's instructions to apply several coats of rub-on finish to back of ornament.

Finishing: Cut out ornament along outer lines. Use glue gun to glue cord to edges of ornament, looping cord at top to form hanger.

Christmas Card Ornaments

You need (for each): Christmas card; poster board; item(s) to decorate ornament – gold cording, ribbons, braids, trims; gold spray paint; glue gun.

Preparing: Cut Christmas card into desired shape. Cut poster board same size; spray paint the back.

Adding hanger: Glue ends of desired trim to back of card.

Finishing: Glue desired trim(s) to card. Glue painted poster board to back of card for backing.

the classic beauty of the Madonna and Child (top) shines on a faux stained-glass ornament created with colorful tissue paper. The exquisite art on last year's greeting cards can be turned into memorable ornaments, too!

*S*imple shapes define these homey
projects. The spicy aroma of gingerbread is
perfect for a kitchen-table Nativity (below).
Use a cookie cutter to create a distinctive
tree-trimmer (right). Homespun fabrics
and basic embroidery stitches (opposite)
create a wall hanging with country appeal.

Cookie Cutter Star

You need: Star-shaped cookie cutter; fabric; paper-backed
fusible web; poster board; button; embroidery floss; needle;
glue gun.

To do: Use web to fuse fabric to poster board. Place cookie
cutter on poster board; trace inner edge of cutter. Cut out
shape just outside drawn line. Use needle and floss to sew
button to center of cutout. Glue cutout inside cutter.

How-To's continued on pages 109-112

the many moods of St. Nick are captured in this cheerful collection! A jolly character, our Santa doll is simple to sew, and kids will have fun constructing the Kris Kringle letter box. For holiday nostalgia, create a fur-clad centerpiece Santa (following page), hand-tinted greeting cards, or our needlepoint pillow.

santa collection

Jolly Santa Doll

Size: 22" tall, top to toe

You need: 60"W parachute fabric – ½ yd red, ¼ yd white; velvet – ½ yd green, ⅛ yd black; 3" x 6½" peach fabric; 3" x 6" gold felt; stuffing; cosmetic blush; two ½" black dome buttons or black embroidery floss; glue stick; shiny red shoelace; 20" dowel.

Cutting fabrics: Enlarge patterns (page 113). Before cutting out, add ¼" seam allowance all around. *From red –* Cut one nose, one jacket front, one 5" x 30" jacket "skirt," and one pair each of hat, jacket back, jacket sleeve, trousers. *From white –* Cut one pom-pom, one hair, one 3" x 16" hatband, one pair of mustaches, and one pair of beards. *From green –* Cut two pairs mittens (four pieces) and one 10" x 22" sack. *From black –* Cut two pairs of boots (four pieces) and one 2½" x 23" belt. *From peach –* Cut one face. *From gold –* Cut two belt buckles.

Stitching: *Stitch pieces with right sides facing unless directed otherwise.* *Trousers –* Pin pieces together; stitch front and back seams. Press seams flat; stitch side and inner leg seams. Set aside. *Boots –* Stitch pairs of boots together. *Trousers/boots –* Gather bottom of each trouser leg to 7". Slip trouser leg inside boot; slipstitch together. Set aside. *Jacket –* Stitch front pieces together. Stitch front to back; set aside. *Sleeves (each) –* Bring sides of sleeve together, notches matching; pin/stitch. Turn right side out. Gather wrist to 5¾"; set aside. *Mittens (each) –* Stitch pieces together; turn. Slip sleeve inside mitten; slipstitch together. *Jacket sleeves –* Set each sleeve in arm opening of jacket; pin/stitch. *Jacket "skirt" –* Fold under ends of strip, then fold in half lengthwise. Starting at jacket front, pin "skirt" around bottom, taking two small pleats at each side as you go; stitch. *Jacket/trousers –* Pin/stitch jacket to trousers, leaving a 4" opening at back (dash line on pattern) for turning. *Head –* Pin/stitch hair and face together end to end, forming a loop. Pin/stitch head to neck of jacket, leaving an opening at front to insert beard (dash line on pattern).

How-To's continued on pages 113-114

Santa Centerpiece

You need: *Santa* – 16"H plastic foam cone; 4¼"H porcelain Santa head; 3¼"L porcelain hands; fabrics – ¾ yd for robe, ½ yd for coat and hat; cotton batting; two 3½" lengths of ½"W velvet ribbon to match robe fabric; white wool doll hair; white fake fur; jingle bell; 18-gauge floral wire; black fabric dye; liner paintbrush; lightweight cardboard. *Bag* – muslin fabric; liquid fabric stiffener; red spray paint; aluminum foil; light red acrylic paint; paintbrush; ½ yd jute twine. *Decorations* – 9"H artificial evergreen tree; miniature pipe; small boxes or pieces of floral foam; wrapping paper; curling ribbon; excelsior; artificial holly sprigs; artificial snow; stuffing. *Other tools* – wire cutters; low-temp glue gun; craft knife; drawing compass.

Making Santa body: Use craft knife to cut 4" from tip of cone; discard tip. With one long edge even with bottom of cone, wrap a 10" x 16" batting piece around cone, leaving top of cone exposed.

How-To's continued on page 115

Tinted Santa Card

You need: Plain note card and envelope; colored pencils; glossy wood-tone floral spray; craft glue; spray adhesive.

Coloring illustration: Photocopy illustration (page 114). Use colored pencils to color copied illustration. Lightly spray with wood-tone spray.

Making card: Trim illustration to fit note card. Use spray adhesive to glue illustration to note card.

How-To's on pages 116-117

country charm

it's comfortable. It's colorful. It's a cozy country Christmas! Holiday touches are easy to add around the room with an abundance of charming checks. For a playful way to mark each place setting, fill tiny watering cans with berries and greenery.

beautiful bows are a quick and simple way to lend cheer to Yuletide dining. For an evergreen accent at the windows (from top left), *tie crimson ribbon into a bow around curtain tabs and tuck sprigs of pine into each knot. Gingham bows create a fresh, festive look atop ivy topiaries or on mason jars filled with white roses.*

Muslin Snowmen

You need (for each): ¼ yd muslin; stuffing; orange polymer clay; sandwich bag; 1 cup clean sand; 2 twigs; cloves; fabric paint – white, black; waterbased varnish; cardboard; paintbrushes; toothpick; glue gun.

Cutting fabric: On paper, draw a freehand snowman, up to 9" tall; add ⅜" seam allowance. Cut out. Fold muslin in half; trace pattern onto muslin; cut out two.

Assembling: Pin pieces together; stitch, leaving openings at sides (arms) and at bottom (base). Clip curves; turn. Stuff, leaving bottom unstuffed. Fill sandwich bag with sand; knot. Insert bag at base; stuff until firm. Stand snowman upright on cardboard; trace bottom; cut shape. Cut muslin ½" larger than cardboard; wrap around cardboard; glue edges. Stitch base to snowman (through muslin). Glue twig arms in place.

Painting: Paint snowman white.

Features: Make nose of clay. Break toothpick into ½"L pieces; insert ¼" in back of nose. Bake clay according to manufacturer's instructions. Poke hole in face; glue toothpick in hole. Dot black paint for eyes and mouth. Glue cloves to chest.

Finishing: Apply two coats of varnish to snowman.

Pinecone Star

You need: 8" x 1½" plastic foam disk; moss-green floral-color spray; craft glue; five Norway-spruce cones; five ponderosa-pinecones; 15 miniature black-and-white spruce cones; 15 pods; spruce, juniper, and pine boughs; one 4"L green chenille stem.

Assembling: Spray disk with floral color; let dry. Glue Norway-spruce cones to top of foam so they extend 3" past disk edges. Glue ponderosa cones between Norway cones, leaving 2½" circle uncovered in center. Glue miniature cones and pods to fill circle. Glue boughs to fill spaces between cones. Glue chenille stem into back of disk for hanger.

To celebrate nature's wintry charm, a rugged pinecone star stands out against a backdrop of fragrant naturals. Folksy figures (opposite) such as our muslin snow family are grouped for a winsome tabletop display.

a *captivating character (right), our papier-mâché Santa is fun to make using a foam cone foundation. Assorted woodsy materials are arranged on a ready-made plaque to convey rustic season's greetings.*

"Happy Holidays" Plaque

You need: Birch plywood plaque; small birch logs; twigs; small grapevine wreath; acrylic paint – red, white, green; paintbrushes; spray acrylic sealer; craft glue; permanent fine-point pen; garden shears; finishing nails; hammer.

Painting: Mark off center of plaque; paint green. Add freehand red and white checks to edge of plaque. Spray with acrylic sealer.

Adding words: Print "Happy Holidays" on front of plaque. Trim twigs to fit words. Glue twigs and wreath over printing.

Adding frame: Nail birch logs to edges of plaque.

Papier-mâché Santa How-To's on page 118

Apple Potpourri

You need: 1 cup dried apple slices; 2 tablespoons ground cinnamon; 1/4 cup whole allspice berries; 10 cinnamon sticks; 2 tablespoons cloves; 1/4 cup canella or nandina berries; 10 small pinecones; 7 drops cinnamon oil; non-metal container with tight-fitting lid.

To do: Combine ingredients in container. Place container in cool, dark, dry place for two weeks. Shake container every few days to mix contents. Add additional oil as needed. You may want to add additional apple slices when displaying the potpourri.

Scented Ginger Garland

You need: Cinnamon; applesauce; gingerbread-man cookie cutter; eye pins; rolling pin; wire rack; narrow cord.

Making dough: Mix 3/4 cup warm applesauce and 1 1/4 cups cinnamon together to form a ball. Roll out to 1/8" thickness.

Making gingerbread ornaments: Using cookie cutter, cut out desired number of ornaments. Push eye pin into top of each head. Place ornaments on wire rack in oven at 150 degrees or lowest setting for 6 to 8 hours with oven door ajar until completely dry.

Making garland: String one ornament onto cord; knot cord at eye pin. Continue stringing and knotting ornaments.

How-To's continued on pages 118-119

the natural aromas (top left) *of the holidays — apple, cinnamon, allspice, and others — are combined in our pretty homemade potpourri. A whimsical garland* (left) *is created with sweet-scented dough that's cut into gingerbread men and dried in the oven, or you can make 3-D "gingerbread" ornaments using paper-covered cardboard. Whether he's formed from gingerbread dough or painted wood, our smiling skater* (above) *captures the spirit of winter fun!*

snow pals

e*ven if no snowflakes fall this year, it's a snap to conjure up frosty friends! A cute snowman candle holder* (right) *can be hand painted in just minutes. Stitch a whole snow pal family* (below), *complete with a snow cat, for a folksy extra. Cross-stitched mitten ornaments* (opposite) *bring a snowy touch to the tree.*

Frosty Family

You need: 1 yd natural cotton batting; 22" x 12" piece of knit fabric; black thread; stuffing; small amount orange polymer clay; 8 small buttons; 10 small twigs; ¼ yd of ¼"W ribbon; small flat-back faux gemstones; glue gun.

Cutting: Use full-size patterns (page 122) to cut two snowman pieces, two snow-woman pieces, four snow-child pieces, and two snow-cat pieces from batting. Cut four 6" x 5½" hats from knit fabric.

Embroidering: On one piece of each snow-person pair, embroider eyes with two strands of thread.

Assembling: Pin pairs of body pieces together, wrong sides facing; blanket-stitch with black thread around edges, leaving top edges open. Stuff; stitch openings closed with blanket stitches. For each hat, fold fabric in half crosswise, right sides facing. Pin and stitch long edge to form tube; stitch curve on one end to form top of hat. Trim fabric near stitching; turn. Fold up ½" twice on lower edge of hat for cuff; glue hats on snow-people.

Finishing: Shape four small "carrot" noses from clay; bake according to manufacturer's instructions. Glue noses to faces. Glue buttons to front of each snow-person. Glue twig arms into side seams. Glue ribbon collar around cat's neck; glue gems to collar.

Snowman Candle Holder

You need: Frosted-glass round votive candle holder; dimensional-paint writers – orange, black; 6" of ⅞"W plaid ribbon; craft glue.

Making holder: Paint black squares on candle holder for eyes and black dots for mouth. Paint an orange triangle for nose. Make knot in center of ribbon. Clip each end of ribbon for fringe. Glue knot of ribbon to candle holder.

Mitten Ornaments How-To's on pages 120-121

a season for stitching

Spread the joyous feeling of the holidays throughout your home with nostalgic cross-stitched creations! Adorn the tree or a package with a vibrant poinsettia ornament (right). Winsome mini stockings featuring a snowman, Santa Claus, or a wintry scene add a Christmasy touch to a mantel or doorknob. A portrait of jolly old Saint Nick toting his toy-filled sack (opposite) lends an eye-catching decorative touch.

How-To's on pages 124-125 and 127

How-To's on page 123

these merry projects are sure to kindle holiday spirits! The silhouette of everyone's favorite gift-giver (below) takes flight across a festive throw pillow. Other familiar symbols and patterns (opposite) appear on lodge-look sweatshirts for him and her. Homespun bread cloths, nice for presenting your baked treats, are quick to stitch, and our framed sampler makes a nostalgic gift.

How-To's on page 126

How-To's on pages 127-130

all the trimmings

dazzle friends and family with your gaily trimmed tree! They'll be delighted with a host of angels, or you can create a glittery setting with shining ornaments. If your tastes run to country, craft a whimsical picket fence, or mix and match these ideas. Set your imagination free to express your own exceptional style!

1.

3.

2.

Trimming the tree is fun — and easy! *1.* Let a little tree shine with store-bought papier-mâché stars spritzed with gold. *2.* Create a country-fresh garland: fuse homespun fabric to poster board and cut into star shapes, then thread them along with painted bottle caps onto paper wire. *3.* Bake jolly sugar cookie characters and tie onto a length of checked ribbon. *4.* For a woodsy look, tuck feather birds, lightly gilded naturals, and tufts of cotton batting "snow" between the branches; ring the tree with natural grapevine. *5.* Shape a big raffia bow and glue on a wooden heart in the center. *6.* Glass ornaments become cosmic baubles when you draw stars with a gold paint pen. *7.* Use a calligraphy pen to write Yuletide messages on parchment paper to nestle in the tree; singe the edges and crumple for a time-worn look. *8.* Coat tree-shaped cookies with colored icing, then decorate with colorful non-pareils and hang with ribbon.

31

angels on high

nestled high among the Christmas tree branches, this
chorus of heavenly ornaments will bring a joyous note to
your holiday decor. An adorable tea-dyed angel, dressed
in velvet and lace, bears a button-trimmed heart.

Tea-dyed Angel

You need: 1/4 yd of linen fabric; tea bag; 7" square of beige or tan velvet; 10" square of off-white moiré; stuffing; acrylic paint for eyes and mouth; cream blush for cheeks, 6" of 1 1/2"W lace; 3" of 3/4"W lace; 7" of 3/8"W gathered lace; small buttons for heart; 24" of 1/8"W off-white ribbon; 2 1/2" grapevine wreath; fabric glue; glue gun.

Dyeing fabric: Dye linen by soaking it in tea (one tea bag to two cups water) for 10 minutes. Dry and press.

Cutting: Add 1/4" seam allowance to full-size patterns (pages 131-133). Cut out as follows: From tea-dyed linen, cut two dolls, four arms, four legs, and one heart. From velvet, cut one dress and one heart. From moiré, cut two wings.

Angel: Pin/stitch each arm and leg. Clip seams at arrows indicated on patterns. Turn, stuff, and stitch closed each arm and leg. (Leg seams face front and back.) With right sides facing, pin/stitch one doll to velvet dress at neckline. Fold dress down over linen. Baste arms and legs in place on doll front. With right sides facing (arms and legs inside, "sandwiched" between), pin/stitch doll back to velvet front; leave opening for turning at bottom. Clip curves at arrows indicated on pattern; turn, stuff, and stitch closed.

Wings: With right sides facing, pin/stitch moiré wings together, leaving opening as shown on pattern. Clip curves at arrows indicated on pattern, turn, and lightly stuff. Stitch closed. Topstitch along wings as indicated by dash lines on pattern. Gather the center of wings and wrap thread around middle to secure. Stitch wings to back of doll as indicated on pattern.

How-To's continued on pages 131-134

*f*or *a sweet touch* (clockwise from bottom left), *make this cute cookie angel and finish it with glazed icing and glittering trims. An old-fashioned clothespin is the foundation for a delicate crocheted angel. Heaven and nature sing for this gilded pinecone angel made with silk-leaf wings and a hazelnut head. So simple to make, our merry muslin angel conveys heartfelt feelings.*

tree time

Create your own heirloom tree with handmade trims you nestle among twinkling lights. It's easy with fanciful felt ornaments — some are shaped like hearts and others like mittens. Slip licorice and gumdrops onto lengths of heavy thread for a yummy garland, or bake up gingerbread ornaments using the recipe on page 85. More magic comes from packing a youngster's gifts in a personalized bushel basket (above) — it can be used to hold other treasures during the year!

Felt Ornaments

You need (for each): Felt; embroidery floss; needle; dimensional-paint writers; ⅛"W ribbon.

Cutting felt: Enlarge desired pattern (page 135) to 6"H. Cut out one pair of felt pieces.

Stitching: Pin cutouts together; join with blanket stitches.

Painting: Follow diagram (page 135), or paint cutout as you please.

Finishing: Thread ornament on ribbon; tie ends together for hanger.

Personalized Bushel Basket

You need: Bushel basket; acrylic paint; wide paintbrush; dimensional-paint writer.

To do: Paint basket inside and out (ribs one color, bands another color). When dry, use dimensional paint to inscribe child's name.

Elegance
from top

to bottom

Simple but splendid, these gilded accents will set your tree all agleam. For a touch of heaven, glue a decorative medallion to a wooden star (opposite), then use metallic paint to create an antiqued look. Make a Victorian-style tree skirt (below) without sewing a stitch — just fuse fabrics to a piece of muslin and finish with painted "stitches."

How-To's on page 135

all that glitters

Shimmers of silver reflect the warm glow of tree lights, candle lanterns, and a crackling fire to light up your home with Yuletide sparkle. Wrap gifts in tones of silver, white, and blue and bind packages with glittery braid, bells, metallic leaves, tulle bows, even paper-clip rings. For brilliant boughs (opposite), slip braided balls among dainty stars, then fill in with storebought icicles and shiny frames. Finish with paper tree chains swinging from branch to branch and a foil dove tree topper to keep watch.

How-To's begin on page 40

top the mantel with spangled topiaries crafted from metallic ball ornaments and painted pinecones.

Sparkling Topiary Tower

You need: About 20 small silver- and gold-painted pinecones; 1" to 2" glass ball ornaments – about 20 shiny silver, 5 matte silver, 4 shiny gold; glue gun; 15"H plastic foam cone; about 30 pearl-head straight pins; small galvanized aluminum bucket; 2½ yds of silver wire-edged ribbon.

Preparing materials: Remove hooks and caps from ornaments; discard hooks.

Making topiary: Glue pinecones, wide sides down, to foam; space cones evenly over foam. Glue ornaments, cap ends down, to fill spaces between cones. Bend sides of ornament caps out to make flowers. Insert pin through center of each flower, then into foam. Place covered cone in bucket. Tie ribbon into bow; glue to top of topiary.

Glimmering Stars

You need (for each): Beads – 70 seed beads #02, ten 5mm beads #02, 6mm miracle beads (two #70, three #40), 5 Czech glass stars #22; 14" of 22-gauge silver-plated wire; heavy-duty scissors.

Making star: Thread beads onto wire as follows – seven seed beads, one 5mm bead, one miracle bead, one 5mm bead, seven seed beads, one star bead; repeat pattern four more times. Form into star shape by bending wire at miracle beads and stars. Twist wire ends together at top of star; trim excess wire.

How-To's continued on pages 136-137

*S*ee your tree magically transformed into a winter
wonderland laced with shining adornments. Straight
from the night sky, wire stars *(from top left) are*
threaded with glimmering beads. Fanciful globes are
a cinch to make by wrapping braid and ribbon around
foam balls. Emblazoned with faux jewels, a chain of
paper trees becomes an enchanting garland.

holiday style

try something different this year — adorn your tree with the icy beauty of snowflakes and the warmth of classic plaids. A striking pinwheel (right) crafted from triangles of ribbon tops the tree in style, and filigree snowflakes (below) can be crocheted in a flurry.

Plaid Pinwheel Tree Topper

You need: 2½ yds of 3"W wire-edged plaid ribbon; 1⅛" gold button; cardboard; drawing compass; wire hanger; craft glue.

Cutting: Use full-size pattern (page 138) to cut 11 triangles from one long edge of ribbon. Use compass to cut a 2½" circle from cardboard and from ribbon.

Gluing: Glue ribbon circle to cardboard circle. Roll triangles into cones; glue. Glue cones to covered cardboard with points to the center. Glue button over cone points. Add hanger.

How-To's continued on pages 137-138

for a fanciful touch (left), use wide plaid ribbon to fashion ball ornaments, colorful nosegays, or simple bows. Children will love the delightful snowman made from a painted wooden clothespin.

folksy and festive

*trimmed with homestyle appeal, this folksy collection captures
the fun and festive spirit of the Yuletide! A parade of picket-fence
Santas renews a bygone tradition of enclosing the base of
the Christmas tree with a decorative fence. Plain wooden
fencing, available in ready-made rolls at garden centers,
is all set to stand in place after you transform it using a
little paint and dabs of spackling compound.*

Santa Picket Fence

You need: 18"H wooden picket fencing; latex paint – red; acrylic paint – peach, pink, black; vinyl spackling compound; light brown waterbase stain; palette knife or craft stick; paintbrushes; matte-finish acrylic spray sealer.

Painting fence: Paint fence with two coats of red latex paint.

Painting each picket: For face, paint a 2"H peach strip 4" below top of picket; paint pink $1/4$-circles for cheeks. Beginning $3^1/2$" from picket top, use palette knife to apply spackling compound around face for hat trim, hair, and beard. Paint black dots for eyes.

Staining: Spray fence with two coats of sealer. Dilute one part stain with one part water. Working on one picket at a time, apply stain to picket; wipe off excess with a soft cloth.

Finishing: Spray fence with one coat of sealer.

Noel and Tree Ornaments

You need (for each): Fabrics – muslin for background, scrap(s) for appliqué(s); paper-backed fusible web; low-loft cotton batting; embroidery floss; embroidery needle; buttons; dressmaker's transfer paper; instant coffee; fabric glue; twig.

Coffee-dyeing fabrics: Dissolve two tablespoons coffee in two cups hot water. Soak fabrics in cooled coffee several minutes. Air-dry fabrics; press.

Preparing background: *Noel* – Cut an approx. $3^1/2$" x $5^1/2$" irregularly shaped rectangle from muslin. Use full-size pattern (page 139) and transfer paper to transfer "NOEL" and greenery only to muslin. *Tree* – Cut an approx. $3^1/2$" x 6" irregularly shaped rectangle from muslin. Use full-size pattern (page 139) and transfer paper to transfer tree trunk and branches only to muslin.

How-To's continued on pages 139-140

turn a plain papier-mâché ornament (from top right) into a celestial tree-trimmer with a painted crescent Santa and star accents. Notions from Mother's sewing basket are the inspiration for the rest of these ornaments embroidered with quaint schoolgirl stitching and a cozy little sweater enhanced with bright, bold buttons.

share the joy

1.

Spread season's greetings with handmade presents and wrappings! Craft elegant jewelry in a snap, or knit a jolly sweater. Delight youngsters with delicious-looking decorations, and welcome friends with tasty treats from your kitchen. All the how-to's follow.

2.

3.

4.

7.

MERRY CHRISTMAS KRISTIN!

8.

Joy

5.

6.

You'll love these no-instructions-needed ideas: **1.** To doll up a plain wrapper, cut a gingerboy shape from a scrap of vinyl flooring, brush with paint, and stamp away! **2.** Surprise a gardener with a pot of seeds and tools. **3.** Gather glass ornaments in a basket; wrap with tulle. **4.** Dip pretzels in melted chocolate, then in sprinkles or nuts. **5.** Use cookie cutters to create potato stamps; let kids decorate their own paper. **6.** Treat Fido to a bow-tied bundle of pet biscuits. **7.** Use sponge circles to paint snowmen on gift wrap and tags. **8.** Hold clean stencils in place and shake powdered sugar on brownies.

cheery checks

a *mosaic of homestyle charm, our country quilt* (opposite) *highlights a cheerful collection of checks! The patchwork medley is a cozy comforter featuring merry motifs such as Christmas trees, rustic stars, jolly snowmen, and quaint stockings. Simple sashing makes the appliquéd blocks easy to assemble. For a coordinating accent to this warming gift, make an extra square such as the pretty poinsettia block* (below) *and turn it into a stylish pillow.*

How-To's on pages 140-144

Cheery Checks Afghan

Finished size: 47" x 81"

You need: Worsted weight yarn – 21 oz (600 gr, 1,440 yds) ecru, 21 oz (600 gr, 1,440 yds) red; crochet hook – size I (5.50 mm) **or** size needed for gauge.

Gauge: 14 dc and 8 rows = 4". *Gauge swatch:* 4¼"W x 4"H – With ecru, ch 17 loosely. Work same as Afghan for 8 rows. Finish off.

AFGHAN

Note: Each row is worked across length of Afghan.

With ecru, ch 207 **loosely**, place marker in last ch made for st placement, ch 2 **loosely:** 209 chs.

Row 1 (Right side)**:** Dc in fourth ch from hook **(3 skipped chs count as first dc)** and in next ch changing to red in last dc (*see* **To Change Colors**, *page 145*), dc in next 3 chs changing to ecru in last dc, ★ dc in next 3 chs changing to red in last dc, dc in next 3 chs changing to ecru in last dc; repeat from ★ across to last 3 chs, dc in last 3 chs: 207 dc.

Note #1: Loop a short piece of yarn around any stitch to mark Row 1 as **right** side.

How-To's continued on page 145

take the chill off winter (opposite) *with our crocheted checked afghan. The cute gingham stocking ornament* (top) *is edged with simple stitches. Bold checks border painted poinsettias on the decorative serving platter.*

personal presents

Stitch up these nifty woollies for grownups and children — just in the "knit" of time! Our sweaters are a snap, even for novices. Dress Santa's little helper (opposite) in North-Pole style with this appliquéd jumper. She'll love the button reindeer!

Tree-and-Snowman Sweater

Size: Women's size small (medium, large). Directions are for smallest size. Directions for larger sizes are in parentheses. If there is only one number, it applies to all sizes. Finished bust size: 44" (48", 52").

You need: Bulky weight yarn – red (900 gms, 31½ oz, 1080 yds), green and white each (100 gms, 3½ oz, 120 yds); knitting needles – 1 pair each sizes 10, 9, and 3; tapestry needle; Persian yarn (8-yd skns) – 1 orange, 1 blue, 1 black; buttons – two ⅜" and three ⅝" black, two ⅝" red, two ¾" blue, three ⅝" gold stars, two ⅝" white stars, two ⅜" white stars, 2 small snowflake stars.

Gauge: In St st with size-10 needles, 11 sts and 14 rows = 4"; check gauge before beginning work.

Back: With size-9 needles and red yarn, cast on 62 (70, 76) sts. Beg with P row, work 3 rows reverse St st, 2 rows St st. Change to size-10 needles. *Row 6 (wrong side):* P2, (k2, p2) across. *Row 7:* K2, (p2, k2) across. Rep last 2 rows for rib twice. Continue in St st until piece measures 13 (14, 14)" from beg. **Shape armholes:** Bind off 4 sts at beg of next 2 rows – 54 (62, 68) sts.

How-To's continued on pages 146-147

Festive Ties

You need (for each): Flannel tie; thick craft glue; embroidery floss; *Santa* – white, light tan, red, green, brown, and black felt; *Snowman* – cotton batting, black felt, flannel (scarf).

Santa tie: Use full-size Santa patterns (page 147) to cut appliqués from felt. Glue appliqués to tie. Open back seam of tie. Use three strands of floss to work blanket stitches as desired along appliqué edges. Restitch seam.

Snowman tie: Use full-size snowman patterns (page 147) to cut appliqués from felt, batting, and flannel. Glue appliqués to tie. Open back seam of tie. Using three strands of floss, work cross stitches for eyes and running stitches for mouth; work blanket stitches along appliqué edges, stopping ⅛" from scarf ends. Fray scarf ends. Restitch seam.

Star-Struck Sneakers

You need: Red sneakers (or paint white sneakers with red fabric paint); gold dimensional fabric-paint writer; 1 yd of ¼"W gold braid; 12" of 1½"W gold ribbon; 12" of 2"W red plaid ribbon; 2 yds of 1½"W red plaid ribbon; fabric glue; glue gun.

Embellishing: *Heel* – Cut 2"W plaid ribbon to fit heel area. Brush fabric glue on sneaker; apply ribbon. *Seams* – Cut gold braid length of each seam (toe and heel); hot-glue braid along seams. *Toe* – From 1½"W gold ribbon, cut out stars (about five per toe) in several sizes. To attach stars, hold to toe with finger and outline star with fabric paint. (Paint acts as glue when dry.) *Instep* – Dot area with gold paint. *Laces* – Cut 1½"W plaid ribbon into two 36"L pieces. Lace sneakers with ribbons.

Put the accent on accessories (clockwise from top left) *with natty neckties for men! Simple stitches enhance the glued-on appliqués. Canvas sneakers take on a festive look with golden stars and ribbon trims, and cross-stitched holiday motifs transform plain gloves into great gifts. Cozy fleece slippers are sewn with love — in no time at all!*

How-To's continued on page 148

Gift-Wrap Romper

You need: Purchased romper (with snap crotch and knit ankle cuffs); about 3 yds of 1½"W wire-edge ribbon; gold dimensional fabric-paint writer; one ¾" gold button.

Preparing romper: Wash and dry romper to insure it is preshrunk and free of sizing; unsnap crotch before you begin.

Attaching ribbon: Turn under one end of ribbon, pin to romper (¼" from neckband), then run the ribbon from the shoulder seam to leg/cuff seam, pinning as you go. Allow ½" for turn-under; cut. Stitch along both sides and ends of ribbon, stitching sides in the same direction   top to bottom. Pin/stitch ribbon across chest (just below underarms) in the same manner.

Making bow: Make a six-looped bow and streamer with leftover ribbon; fold streamer end in a point. Tack bow where ribbons cross; attach button to center.

How-To's continued on pages 148-150

a *wool jacket* (left) *blossoms with Christmas appeal when you add appliquéd poinsettias and embroidered holly. To wrap baby in cheer* (top left), *just stitch ribbon to a romper and tack on a buttoned-up bow! Little girls — and big girls, too! — can spread holiday spirit with the crocheted lollipop lapel pin.*

finishing touches

With just a few dabs of paint, you can add customized accents to table linens and gift wrap and create a grand impression! Lightly pounce fabric paint on purchased linens (opposite) to whip up a set of holiday napkins in no time. Repeat a pattern on gift paper (above) or combine different motifs on packages. Coordinate the presentation with cute stenciled gift tags cut from cardstock using pinking shears, and you'll have the holiday all wrapped up!

Stenciling

You need: Sheet of acetate; craft knife; permanent felt-tip pen; stencil brush; acrylic paint (for stenciling paper) or fabric paint (for stenciling fabric); removable tape; paper towels.

Making stencil: Enlarge stencil pattern (page 150) to desired size. Transfer stencil pattern to acetate using felt-tip pen. Cut out stencil using craft knife.

Stenciling: Secure stencil to surface with tape. Holding stencil brush upright, dip brush into paint; dab on a paper towel to remove excess paint. Pounce almost-dry brush through stencil. Lift stencil straight up when removing.

last-minute gifts

With a little of this, and a little of that, pull together one-of-a-kind presents that no one will ever guess were last-minute! Our stylish pins, embellished with buttons and charms, are created from wrapping-paper cutouts.

Victorian Pins

You need (for each): Wrapping paper with Victorian Santa print; poster board; paper-backed fusible web; clear gloss finish for paper tole; items for decorating pin; glue gun; small scissors; pin back.

Making cutout: Fuse web to wrong side of wrapping paper; remove paper backing. Fuse wrapping paper to poster board. Using scissors, cut out Santa figure. Apply a thick coat of gloss finish; let dry.

Finishing: Decorate by gluing items to cutout. Glue pin back to back of cutout.

"Teacher's Pet" Pot

You need: Terra-cotta pot; acrylic paint – yellow, black, white, red; paintbrushes; acrylic spray sealer.

Painting: *Ruler* – Paint rim of pot yellow. Use black paint to add "ruler" design to rim. *Blackboard* – Paint sides of pot black. Use white and red paint to add designs to sides of pot.

Finishing: Spray pot with sealer.

How-To's continued on page 151

Our *"teacher's pet" pot (clockwise from top left) is an extra-smart gift! Paint the "blackboard" and ruler trim on a terra-cotta pot, then fill with classroom supplies. Dress up store-bought cloth napkins with painted stripes, dots, and stars, or brush jolly snow fellows onto cotton dish towels with fabric paint — wherever you turn, someone smiles back! Lightly sanded, these weathered frames are great for displaying family photos or nostalgic prints.*

59

teddy time

Our huggable bears would love to spend the holidays with your family and friends! A joy to crochet, the cuddly trio is sure to evoke a lighthearted mood. Our teddy-time wreath (opposite) is trimmed with ready-made bears, miniature sleds, shovels, and easy pom-pom "snowballs."

Crocheted Teddy Bear

Size: approx. 14" tall
You need: Sport weight yarn – 7 ounces, (200 grams, 712 yards); crochet hook size B (2.25 mm), or size needed to obtain gauge below; stuffing; 15 mm eyes and 12 x 10 mm nose; 18"of 1"W ribbon.
Gauge: In loop pattern – 24 sts = 4"; 24 rows = 4". Make a swatch to check gauge.

Stitches: *Loop st* – Insert hook into next st, wrap yarn from back to front around left index finger; catch both strands of yarn around index finger; pull yarn through st; slip loop off finger; adjust size of loop by gently pulling yarn. Hold loop in place with middle finger, wrap yarn around hook; draw hook through all 3 lps on hook. **Dec A** – Draw up a lp in each of next 2 sts, yo and draw through all three lps on hook. **Dec B** – Draw up a lp in each of next 3 sts, yo and draw through all 4 lps on hook.

Body (make 2): Ch 6. *Row 1* (right side): Sk 1 ch, 1 sc in each ch to end – 5 sc. *Row 2 and alt rows*: Ch 1, Loop st in each sc to end. *Row 3*: Ch 1, 2 sc in 1st st, 3 sc in each of next 3 sts, 2 sc in last st – 13 sc. *Row 5*: Ch 1, 2 sc in 1st st, (1 sc in next st, 2 sc in next st) twice, 1 sc in each of next 3 sts, (2 sc in next st, 1 sc in next st) twice, 2 sc in last st – 19 sc. *Row 7*: Ch 1,

2 sc in 1st st, ★ 1 sc in each of next 3 sts, 2 sc in next st, 1 sc in each of next 2 sts, 2 sc in next st, rep from ★ once, 1 sc in each of next 3 sts, 2 sc in last st – 25 sc. *Row 9*: Ch 1, 2 sc in 1st st, 1 sc in each of next 5 sts, (2 sc in next st, 1 sc in each of next 3 sts) 3 times, 2 sc in next st, 1 sc in each of next 5 sts, 2 sc in last st – 31 sc. *Row 11*: Ch 1, 1 sc in each st to end. *Row 12*: Rep Row 2. Rep Rows 11 and 12 twelve times. *Row 37*: Ch 1, Dec A, 1 sc in each of next 5 sts, (Dec A, 1 sc in each of next 3 sts) 3 times, Dec A, 1 sc in each of next 5 sts, Dec A – 25 sc. *Row 38 and alt rows*: Rep Row 2. *Row 39*: Ch 1,

How-To's continued on pages 152-153

creations for k1ds

delight the youngsters in your family with delicious-looking decorations and fun-to-create cookies! Gumdrops, licorice, and jelly beans bedeck this sugarplum house (opposite), *a cardboard cottage that's covered with glued-on confections. From lollipops to pinwheel peppermints, quick plastic canvas candies (left) offer four "flavorful" designs. Give a little one a bucketful of fun with our clever Create-A-Cookie Kit! It has everything needed to make festive cookies — from white chocolate cookie dough and edible icing "paints" to a painter's drop cloth and baking instructions.

How-To's on pages 153-155

from your
christmas
kitchen

batches of marvelous munchies and sensational sweets make deliciously easy gifts! The whole family will go nuts over our assortment of six crunchy snacks, ranging from sweet java-flavored pecans to four-alarm almonds.

Espresso Pecans

    4   cups pecans
  1/2   cup water
    1   tablespoon espresso powder
    1   cup confectioners' sugar
  1/2   cup firmly packed light-brown
        sugar
    2   tablespoons coffee liqueur
    2   tablespoons unsalted butter

1. Preheat oven to 350°. Spread pecans on baking sheet. Bake in preheated oven for 8 to 10 minutes or until fragrant. Place in bowl. Spray cooled baking sheet with nonstick vegetable-oil cooking spray.
2. In large nonstick skillet over medium heat, stir together water, espresso powder, confectioners' sugar, brown sugar, and coffee liqueur until dissolved.
3. Bring to boil and cook over medium heat for 5 minutes or until syrupy. Stir in butter and pecans. Simmer for 3 to 4 minutes more or until syrup evaporates and nuts are coated. Turn out onto prepared baking sheet; spread out. Cool completely; store in airtight container for up to 3 weeks.
Yield: Makes 4 cups

Party-Hearty Mix

    4   cups oven-toasted corn-cereal
        squares
    2   cans (1 1/2 ounces each) potato
        sticks
    1   cup honey-roasted peanuts
    3   tablespoons melted butter or
        vegetable oil
    2   tablespoons Worcestershire sauce
    2   tablespoons liquid cayenne-pepper
        sauce
  1/2   teaspoon seasoned salt

1. In 3-quart microwavable bowl, combine cereal, potato sticks, and peanuts.
2. In small bowl, combine melted butter, Worcestershire, cayenne sauce, and seasoned salt; mix well. Pour butter mixture over cereal mixture. Toss to coat evenly.
3. Microwave, uncovered, on HIGH for 6 minutes, stirring well every 2 minutes. Transfer mix to paper towels. Cool completely; store in airtight container.
Yield: Makes about 6 cups

Provençal Rosemary-Nut Mix

  1/2   cup olive oil
    2   cups whole natural almonds
    2   cups walnuts
    5   cloves garlic, minced
    2   tablespoons chopped fresh
        rosemary
  1/2   teaspoon ground cayenne pepper

1. In large skillet over medium heat, combine olive oil, almonds, and walnuts. Cook for 8 minutes, stirring occasionally, until walnuts begin to color. Add garlic, and cook 2 minutes more.
2. Remove skillet from heat; let stand 5 minutes. Stir in rosemary and cayenne. Place nut mixture on baking sheets lined with paper towels to drain excess oil. Cool; store in airtight container for up to 2 weeks.
Yield: Makes 4 cups

Candy-Coated Popcorn

    3   quarts air-popped popcorn
    1   cup peanuts
  1/2   cup salted butter
    1   cup firmly packed light-brown
        sugar
  1/4   cup honey
 1 1/4 teaspoons vanilla
  1/2   teaspoon ground ginger
  1/4   cup toasted sesame seeds

1. Preheat oven to 250°. Line 2 jelly-roll pans with aluminum foil, and spray with nonstick vegetable-oil cooking spray. Spread air-popped popcorn and peanuts on pans.
2. In medium saucepan, combine butter, sugar, and honey. Bring to boil over medium heat, and cook for 5 minutes without stirring. Remove from heat; stir in vanilla, ginger, and sesame seeds. Pour over popcorn and peanuts, stirring to coat.
3. Bake in preheated 250° oven for 1 hour, stirring 3 times during baking. Cool popcorn mixture in pans, then break up clumps. Store in airtight container for up to 2 weeks.
Yield: Makes 12 cups

Spiced-Nuts Glacé

    3   cups unsalted mixed whole nuts
        (about 1 pound)
    1   cup granulated sugar
  1/2   cup firmly packed light-brown
        sugar
  1/2   teaspoon salt
  1/2   teaspoon ground cinnamon
  1/2   teaspoon ground nutmeg
  1/8   teaspoon ground cloves
  1/2   cup light corn syrup
  1/2   cup water
    2   tablespoons unsalted butter or
        margarine

1. Preheat oven to 350°. Spread nuts in jelly-roll pan. Bake in preheated oven for 10 minutes or until hot.
2. Meanwhile, in medium saucepan, combine granulated and brown sugars, salt, cinnamon, nutmeg, cloves, corn syrup, and water. Heat, stirring constantly, over low heat until sugars dissolve; then cook, without stirring, to 300° on candy thermometer. (Syrup will separate into brittle threads when dropped in cold water.)
3. Stir in nuts and butter or margarine until nuts are evenly coated. Spoon into 15 x 10 x 1-inch jelly-roll pan sprayed with nonstick vegetable-oil cooking spray. Spread in even layer, and cool completely.
4. Break glacé into bite-size pieces, and store in tightly covered container for up to 3 weeks.
Yield: Makes about 4 cups

Peppery Almonds

This produces quite a hot mix; adjust the seasonings to taste.

    2   pounds unblanched almonds
  1/2   cup (1 stick) unsalted butter
    1   tablespoon sugar
    1   teaspoon salt
  1/2   teaspoon each ground cayenne
        pepper, ground white pepper,
        and ground black pepper
        Paprika, to taste

1. Preheat oven to 250°.
2. In large skillet over medium-high heat, sauté almonds in butter for 5 minutes or until nuts are coated with melted butter.

Pique the taste buds with gourmet condiments (right). Package **Jalapeño Honey Mustard with Sun-Dried Tomatoes**, **Cranberry-Ginger Vinegar**, and **Bourbon-Spiked Butterscotch Sauce** in sparkling jars. For an unusual breakfast treat (opposite), deliver a crock of **Spiced Pear Butter**.

Transfer almonds and butter in skillet to ungreased jelly-roll pan.

3. In small measuring cup, combine sugar, salt, and cayenne, white, and black peppers. Sprinkle mixture over nuts; stir with wooden spoon to distribute evenly.

4. Bake almond mixture in preheated 250° oven for 35 minutes, stirring every 10 minutes, until toasted. (Check often to prevent burning.)

5. Remove almond mixture from oven; sprinkle with paprika. Place almonds on paper towels to drain excess butter, if desired. Store in airtight container.

Yield: Makes 8 cups

Jalapeño Honey Mustard with Sun-Dried Tomatoes

Because this mustard is spicy-hot, you may wish to use less of it than regular mustard.

- 1 cup dry mustard
- 1/4 cup all-purpose flour
- 1/2 cup water
- 1/2 cup mustard seeds
- 1 cup cider vinegar
- 1 cup honey
- 2 teaspoons salt
- 2 to 4 tablespoons seeded and chopped jalapeño pepper
- 2 to 4 tablespoons chopped oil-packed sun-dried tomatoes (optional)

1. Stir together mustard and flour in a medium saucepan until blended. Whisk in water; let stand 10 minutes.

2. Stir in mustard seeds, vinegar, honey, and salt. Bring to simmering over medium heat, whisking constantly; cook 2 minutes. Remove from heat. Stir in jalapeño and tomatoes, if using. Scrape into sterilized decorative glass jars. Refrigerate for up to 2 months.

Yield: Makes 3 1/3 cups

Bourbon-Spiked Butterscotch Sauce

- 3/4 cup dark corn syrup
- 1 cup firmly packed light-brown sugar
- 1/4 cup heavy cream
- 1/4 cup (1/2 stick) unsalted butter
- 1 to 2 tablespoons bourbon
- 1/2 teaspoon vanilla
  Pinch salt

1. Combine syrup, sugar, cream, and butter in saucepan.

2. Bring to simmering; cook 1 minute. Remove from heat.

3. Stir in bourbon, vanilla, and salt. Cool. Skim top; pour into sterilized jars. Refrigerate for up to 1 month.

Yield: Makes 2 1/4 cups

Cranberry-Ginger Vinegar

Our recipe for a tangy cranberry salad dressing follows.

- 1 pound fresh or frozen cranberries, chopped
- 4 slices peeled fresh gingerroot
- 4 cups distilled white vinegar
- 1 cup water
- 1/4 cup honey

1. Combine all ingredients in non-aluminum medium saucepan. Bring to simmering over medium heat. Remove from heat. Let stand, uncovered, overnight.

2. Strain through fine-mesh sieve, pressing solids to extract all juices. Pour into sterilized jars or decorative bottles. Refrigerate for up to 3 months.

Yield: Makes 5 cups

Cranberry-Ginger Vinaigrette

Whisk together 1/4 cup Cranberry-Ginger Vinegar, 1/2 cup olive oil, 1 teaspoon Dijon-style mustard, 1/2 teaspoon salt, and dash liquid red-pepper seasoning until blended. Refrigerate.

Spiced Pear Butter

- 6 pounds ripe pears, peeled and cored
- 2 tablespoons cider vinegar
- 2 cups firmly packed light-brown sugar
- 2/3 cup honey
- 2 teaspoons grated lemon rind
- 1/4 cup fresh lemon juice
- 1/2 teaspoon ground allspice

1. Wash half-pint canning jars, bands, and lids in hot, soapy water. Rinse. Place jars, bands, and lids in pot of water. Bring to boiling. Keep simmering until ready to use.

2. Working in batches, purée pears in blender or food processor. Transfer purée to large Dutch oven. Stir in vinegar, sugar, honey, lemon rind, lemon juice, and allspice.

3. Bring to boiling; cook, uncovered, for 25 minutes, stirring occasionally (see Note). Reduce heat to medium; gently boil 40 to 45 minutes more until jam-like consistency, stirring more frequently as mixture thickens. Butter is cooked when path made by a wooden spoon pulled through the butter takes about 5 seconds to close.

4. Ladle butter into sterilized half-pint jars from Step 1, leaving 1/4-inch headspace. Cover with hot, clean lids; screw on bands firmly. Process in boiling water bath for 5 minutes. Cool jars on wire rack. Test seals. Label, date, and store in cool (60°), dark place for up to 1 year.

Note: As the butter cooks, you may wish to cover the pot partially, to prevent spattering.

Yield: Makes 4 half-pint jars

sweet little gifts

miniature morsels
prove that good things
come in small packages!
Irresistible bite-size
Party Petits Fours
(right) *have rich chiffon
centers covered with
flavored frosting.*

Party Petits Fours

*Start with a rich chiffon cake that you can
make a day or two ahead, then frost and
decorate.*

Chiffon Cake:

- 2$^1/_4$ cups sifted cake flour
- 1$^1/_4$ cups granulated sugar
- 1 tablespoon baking powder
- $^1/_2$ teaspoon salt
- 2 eggs, separated
- $^1/_3$ cup vegetable oil
- 1 cup milk
- 1 teaspoon vanilla

Flavored Icing:

- 2 cups strawberry-flavored
   confectioners' sugar
- 2 cups chocolate-flavored
   confectioners' sugar
- 2 cups plain confectioners' sugar
- 9 tablespoons water

Buttercream Frosting:
- ½ cup (1 stick) butter or margarine, at room temperature
- 1 box (1 pound) sifted confectioners' sugar
- 3 to 4 tablespoons water
  Pinch salt
  Assorted food colorings

1. Chiffon Cake: Preheat oven to 350°. Grease 15 x 10 x 1-inch baking pan; line bottom with waxed paper; grease paper.
2. Sift cake flour, 1 cup of the granulated sugar, baking powder, and salt into large bowl.
3. In medium bowl, beat egg whites until foamy and doubled in volume; sprinkle in remaining ¼ cup granulated sugar, 1 tablespoon at a time, beating constantly until soft peaks form.
4. Blend oil and ½ cup of the milk into flour mixture; beat 1 minute with mixer at medium speed. Stir in yolks, remaining ½ cup milk, and vanilla; beat 1 minute at medium speed. Fold in egg-white mixture until no streaks of white remain. Pour into prepared pan.
5. Bake in preheated 350° oven 30 minutes, or until top of cake springs back when pressed lightly with fingertip.
6. Cool in pan on wire rack 5 minutes; loosen cake around edges with knife; invert onto large rack or clean towel; peel off waxed paper; let cake cool completely. Wrap in airtight container and store refrigerated up to 2 days, or double wrap and freeze up to 2 weeks.
7. When ready to frost and decorate, unwrap cake and place on cutting board, trim crusts. Cut cake into small diamonds, rectangles, squares, and 1½-inch rounds, as pictured (see page 68).
8. Flavored Icing: For each flavor, whisk together 2 cups of corresponding confectioners' sugar with 3 tablespoons water until smooth.
9. Brush crumbs off cake pieces using soft, dry pastry brush. Place cakes on wire racks set over waxed-paper-lined baking sheets.
10. Spoon Flavored Icing over cakes, coating sides and tops (see Note).
11. Buttercream Frosting: Cream butter in medium bowl; gradually beat in sugar, water, and salt until frosting is creamy smooth.

12. To decorate, tint small amounts of Buttercream Frosting. Spoon into pastry bags; pipe on as pictured (see page 68). Let air-dry on racks. Store in airtight container up to 1 week.
Note: To reuse Flavored Icing, press it through fine-mesh sieve to strain out crumbs.
Yield: Makes 6½ dozen cakes

Christmas Candy Bark

- 6 squares (6 ounces) white baking chocolate
- 1 cup (5 ounces) red and green jelly-candy rings (Chuckles), diced into ⅜-inch pieces

1. Spray baking sheet lightly with nonstick vegetable-oil cooking spray. In heavy saucepan over low heat, melt chocolate, stirring until smooth. Stir in jelly-candy pieces.
2. Scrape onto prepared baking sheet, spreading level. Cool until hardened. Cut into irregular shapes with sharp knife, and store in airtight container in cool place for up to 2 weeks.
Yield: Makes about ¾ pound

Tiger Butter

- 1 cup milk-chocolate chips
- 2 cups white morsels
- 2 cups peanut-butter chips
- ½ cup chopped unsalted peanuts

1. Line jelly-roll pan with foil. In separate small saucepans over low heat, or in small bowls in microwave oven, melt 3 types of chips, stirring until smooth.
2. Pour melted peanut-butter chips into prepared pan, spreading level. Sprinkle on peanuts. Pour melted white morsels and chocolate chips on top, drizzling each randomly.
3. To marbleize, use knife to pull through chocolate in wide curves. Refrigerate until set; break into squares.
Yield: Makes 2 pounds

*these tasty tidbits include something for everyone on your gift list! Diced jelly-candy rings give **Christmas Candy Bark** (from left, in container) its Christmasy colors. Marbled **Tiger Butter** blends three kinds of chips with peanuts. Chopped almonds accent **Chocolate-Topped Toffee**.*

*Chocolate-Dipped Dried Fruits (right) offer an assortment of sweet, semisweet, and marbleized coatings. Pretty little **Pumpkin-Walnut Rings** (opposite, from top) are seasoned with sweet spices and glazed with white chocolate. Two popular snacks are combined for **Pistachio-and-Popcorn Brittle**. Try a twist on the traditional with **Orange Fruitcakes**, full of pecans and dried cranberries.*

Chocolate-Topped Toffee

     1   cup firmly packed light-brown
         sugar
    1/2 cup water
    1/2 cup (1 stick) unsalted butter
    1/2 cup blanched almonds, finely
         chopped
     1   teaspoon vanilla
     1   cup semisweet milk-chocolate
         chips or white morsels
     1   cup blanched almonds, lightly
         toasted and finely chopped

1. Generously butter 1 baking sheet. In medium heavy saucepan, mix sugar, water, and butter. Cook over medium heat, stirring often, until mixture reaches 280° on candy thermometer. Remove from heat; stir in 1/2 cup almonds and vanilla.

2. Pour hot mixture onto baking sheet. Spread with metal spatula to 1/4-inch thickness; immediately scatter chocolate chips over hot toffee, pressing chips lightly so they start melting. When chocolate is soft, spread it evenly over toffee.

3. Top toffee with remaining nuts. Cool; break into pieces. Store, refrigerated, in airtight container for up to 3 weeks.
Yield: Makes about 1 pound 6 ounces

Chocolate-Dipped Dried Fruits

     4   ounces German sweet chocolate,
         chopped
     6   ounces semisweet chocolate,
         chopped
     6   ounces imported white chocolate,
         chopped
         Assorted dried fruits (apricots,
         peach or pear halves, and dates)

1. In separate small saucepans over low heat, or in small bowls in microwave oven, melt 3 types of chocolates, stirring until smooth. Insert toothpick into each fruit to be dipped.

2. Dip some fruit into dark and some into white chocolates. (To marbleize, mix small amounts of dark and white chocolates; swirl together.) Cover at least half of each fruit; let excess drip off. Place fruit on waxed paper.

3. Let stand or refrigerate on tray for 30 minutes, until chocolate is firm. Drizzle with additional melted chocolate, if desired; let set until hardened. Store, refrigerated, in airtight container for up to 3 weeks.
Yield: Makes about 24 pieces

Pumpkin-Walnut Rings

    1 1/4 cups sifted cake flour
     1   teaspoon baking soda
     1   teaspoon ground cinnamon
    1/4 teaspoon ground nutmeg
    1/4 teaspoon ground cloves
    1/4 teaspoon salt
    1/2 cup coarsely chopped walnuts
     2   large eggs
    3/4 cup firmly packed light-brown
         sugar
    1/4 cup vegetable oil
     1   cup canned unsweetened pumpkin
         purée

White-Chocolate Glaze:
     3   ounces imported white chocolate
     1   tablespoon vegetable oil
         Chopped walnuts, for garnish

1. Preheat oven to 350°. Grease and flour six 1-cup baby Bundt pans or one 6-cup Bundt pan.
2. Combine flour, baking soda, cinnamon, nutmeg, cloves, salt, and walnuts in medium bowl. Stir to blend. Set aside.
3. Beat together eggs, brown sugar, and oil in large bowl with electric mixer about 2 to 3 minutes or until very smooth. Add pumpkin purée. Beat until smooth. Add flour mixture; beat just until blended. Spoon batter evenly into prepared pans (or large pan).
4. Bake in preheated 350° oven 20 minutes for 1-cup pans (30 to 35 minutes for 6-cup pan), or until wooden pick inserted in thickest part of cake comes out clean. Let cool in pans on wire rack 10 minutes, then invert cakes onto rack to cool completely.
5. Glaze: Break white chocolate into 1/2-inch pieces. Place in top of double boiler along with oil over hot, but not simmering, water. Stir frequently until chocolate melts and mixture is smooth. Remove upper part of double boiler; set in bowl of ice water. Stir often, until glaze thickens enough for small amount to pool when dropped from spoon onto surface. Spoon glaze over top of each cake, allowing to drip over sides; sprinkle on chopped walnuts.
Yield: Makes 6 small Bundt cakes or 1 large cake

Pistachio-and-Popcorn Brittle

1½ cups shelled pistachios
1 cup coarsely crumbled, popped (preferably without oil), unsalted fresh popcorn
1½ cups sugar
½ cup light corn syrup
½ cup water
3 tablespoons unsalted butter
1 teaspoon salt
¼ teaspoon baking soda
1 teaspoon vanilla

1. Preheat oven to 250°. Butter 15½ x 10½ x 1-inch jelly-roll pan. Spread whole pistachios and popcorn in prepared pan.
2. Bake in preheated 250° oven 5 minutes. Turn off oven but leave pan inside.
3. Combine sugar, corn syrup, and water in large saucepan. Bring to boiling over medium heat. Wipe down any sugar crystals from sides of pan with pastry brush dipped in cold water. When mixture boils, add butter. Cook, stirring occasionally, until candy thermometer registers 310°. Remove from heat. Immediately stir in salt, baking soda, and vanilla. Add warm nuts and popcorn; stir in quickly.
4. Spread candy as thinly and evenly as possible in pan, flattening with nylon or wooden spatula; don't be concerned about gaps or irregular edges. Let brittle cool and harden.
5. Break brittle into chunks. Let cool completely. Store at room temperature in airtight canister or jar.
Yield: Makes 16 servings

Orange Fruitcakes
Cake:
2 cups all-purpose flour
1 teaspoon baking powder
½ teaspoon baking soda
¾ teaspoon ground cinnamon
¼ teaspoon salt
¼ teaspoon ground nutmeg
1 cup pecans, coarsely chopped
¾ cup glacéed cherries, halved
½ cup golden raisins
½ cup diced candied orange peel
½ cup dried cranberries

1 tablespoon grated orange rind
½ cup (1 stick) unsalted butter
1½ cups sugar
2 eggs
¾ cup buttermilk

Orange Syrup:
⅓ cup strained orange juice
2 tablespoons honey
2 tablespoons orange liqueur (optional)
Apricot jam
Candied cherries, coarsely chopped
Candied orange rind

1. Preheat oven to 350°. Line 24 muffin cups with foil muffin liners; spray lightly with nonstick vegetable-oil cooking spray.
2. Stir flour, baking powder, baking soda, cinnamon, salt, and nutmeg in medium bowl until well mixed. Combine pecans, cherries, raisins, orange peel, cranberries, and orange rind in another bowl. Stir a few tablespoons flour mixture into pecan mixture to coat ingredients.
3. Beat together butter and sugar in large bowl until smooth and creamy. Beat in eggs, 1 at a time, until light and fluffy, about 2 minutes. Stir in flour mixture alternately with buttermilk until blended, beginning and ending with flour mixture. Gently stir in pecan mixture. Spoon batter (scant ¼ cupfuls) into prepared muffin cups, dividing evenly.
4. Bake in preheated 350° oven until wooden pick inserted in center comes out clean, about 20 minutes.
5. Meanwhile, make Orange Syrup: Stir together orange juice, honey, and liqueur, if you wish, in bowl until blended.
6. When cakes are done, remove from oven. Let stand in pans on wire rack 10 minutes. Remove from pans. Prick holes in cakes with long-tined fork; brush syrup over cakes. Let cool. Store in airtight containers, in cool place, up to 2 weeks.
7. To decorate, brush with apricot jam; top with candied cherries and orange rind.
Yield: Makes 24 individual fruitcakes

festive traditions

Welcoming wreaths, glowing candles, stockings hung by the chimney with care ... such traditions bring an air of festivity to the season. Enjoy the fast-fix ideas here, or fashion the sensational displays on the following pages.

1.

2.

3.

1. Write a holiday message on a ready-made canvas stocking that you fuse with fabric hearts; glue on button extras. **2.** Whipstitch kraft paper stocking cutouts together; fill with fragrant herbs for easy place cards. **3.** Take tiny twig wreaths, tuck in or glue on berries, dried flowers, and other accents; use as ornaments to trim the tree or string together to brighten a window. **4.** Set star-shaped candles afloat in a pretty bowl atop a starry pewter charger. **5.** Cut-glass holders lend elegance to a grouping of tapers. **6.** Reward Santa with stockings of his own: brightly iced cookies! **7.** Add country charm to a vine wreath in no time! Wire on cheery checked bows and trees cut from painted foam core board, and tuck in berry sprigs.

Berry and Bay Wreath

You need: 20" wire wreath; eucalyptus; bay leaves; pepper berries; dried pomegranates; floral wire; glue gun.

To do: Wire eucalyptus and bay leaves to wreath. Glue pepper berries and pomegranates to greens.

Fragrant Fancy Wreath

You need: 20" wire wreath; cedar; lemon leaves; cinnamon sticks; star anise; lavender; purple grape berries; floral wire; glue gun.

To do: Wire cedar to wreath in a clockwise direction. Glue six long cinnamon sticks and sprigs of lavender together. Glue six small cinnamon sticks together; glue a star anise on top. Glue this to larger bundle; glue to wreath. Glue lemon leaves to wreath; glue star anise randomly to leaves. Tuck in purple grape berries; glue.

Jolly Holly Wreath

You need: 20" wire wreath; boxwood; juniper; silk holly leaves with berries; 10 yds of 1"W red gingham ribbon; floral wire; glue gun.

To do: Wire greens in one direction to wreath. Glue holly and berries to greens. Tie bows; glue to wreath.

Welcome one and all with wonderful wreaths! Scarlet berries and pomegranates glow amid a circlet of eucalyptus and bay leaves (opposite). *Create a fragrant fancy* (top) *with lavender, lemon leaves, and cinnamon sticks among layers of cedar. For holly-jolly fun, simply add gingham bows to a wreath of boxwood, juniper, and holly* (left).

let it glow

Set the mood with gently flickering candles! Aromatic greenery adorns an antique candle holder (left); the flame's warmth releases the fragrance of the leaves. For a glowing centerpiece (below), nest votives in hollowed-out apples, then tuck into a pan lined with greenery and nuts.

bright lights (from top left):
Glue cinnamon sticks,
grapefruit slices, or
dried flowers and herbs to
candles and dip in wax to seal.
Turn to holly berries, sprigs of
spruce, and gingham bows
to transform antique spools
into charming candlesticks.
Clove-studded votives wear
wreaths of cedar roses, pepper
berries, or dried orange slices.

How-To's on page 156

stockings to hang

Surprise Saint Nick with this fun lineup of stockings! You'll jingle all the way (opposite) with the fun jester styles that feature zigzag cuffs and tiny bells. Let your favorite little elves follow our simple how-to's to create the cheery felt stockings (below) decorated with bright stars and hearts. They're fast to assemble using embroidery floss and running stitches.

Jester Stockings

You need (for each): Fabrics – ½ yd main fabric, ½ yd lining fabric, ¼ yd cuff fabric; 8 jingle bells.

Cutting: Enlarge patterns (page 156). From main fabric, cut two stocking sections and one 2" x 6" hanging-loop section. From lining fabric, cut two stocking sections. From cuff fabric, cut two cuff sections.

Sewing: *All stitching is done with ¼" seams, right sides facing and raw edges even, unless otherwise noted.* Stitch fabric stocking sections together, leaving upper edge open. Clip curves; turn. Stitch lining sections together in same way; also leave 6" opening along back edge.

How-To's continued on page 156

eat, drink, and be merry

make the most of holiday time by inviting friends and family for festive open houses, elegant dinners, and casual gatherings. Set out plates of scrumptious cookies to delight drop-in guests, or toast the season with spirited beverages. We'll show you how to liven up your holiday table with the "instant" ideas here!

1.

2.

3.

4.

7.

8.

5.

These special touches are simple to do: *1. For creative drink swizzlers, tie sticks of peppermint and cinnamon together and add fresh mint. 2. Tie napkins with raffia; trim with bells, stars, and pinecones. 3. Use alphabet cookie cutters and your favorite recipe to spell out any greeting of your choice. 4. Stitch little velvet bags, fill with trinkets, and cinch with gold ribbon. 5. To ring in the season with merriment, slip bells onto wire loops; tie onto goblets with gold cord. 6. Hand-write your menu and mount it on foil wrapping paper, then glue to colored paper; complete with a silvery bow. 7. Fill tiny terra-cotta pots with moss and top with lady apples for place-card holders (cut slits to hold the cards). 8. With a new paintbrush, apply icing and diluted paste food coloring to a special cookie just for Santa!*

6.

Welcome friends and family to the most joyous of seasons by lifting a chill-chasing cup of wintry cheer! For coffee with an interesting twist, try almond-flavored **Vanilla Cappuccino** (from top left) and minty **Mocha Warmer**. Or toast the holiday with **Caroler's Cider** and **Cranberry Tea**, accented with sticks of cinnamon or peppermint for stirring.

Vanilla Cappuccino

  1 box (5 individual envelopes) vanilla cappuccino
  5 cups hot (not boiling) water
$^1/_3$ cup amaretto liqueur (or almond extract to taste)
     Freshly grated nutmeg or ground cinnamon, for garnish (optional)

1. Empty contents of envelopes into 8-cup heatproof server.
2. Add hot water and stir until well combined. Stir in amaretto liqueur or almond extract.
3. Pour cappuccino mixture into small cups or, if drink is made without liqueur, glass mugs. Dust tops with nutmeg or cinnamon, if you wish.
Yield: Makes 10 half-cup servings

toast
the season

Caroler's Cider

- 3 cups water
- 4 cinnamon-apple-flavored tea bags, individual size
- 1/4 cup seedless red raspberry jam
- 2 cups apple cider or apple juice
  Cinnamon sticks

1. Heat water to boiling in medium-size saucepan. Remove from heat. Add tea bags; cover and steep for 5 minutes. Remove tea bags.
2. Add raspberry jam to tea and stir until dissolved. Stir in apple cider. Reheat.
3. Pour into teacups or mugs and add cinnamon sticks as stirrers.
Yield: Makes 10 half-cup servings

Cranberry Tea

- 3 cups water
- 4 cinnamon-flavored tea bags, individual size
- 2 tablespoons honey (or to taste)
- 2 cups cranberry drink
  Small candy canes or cinnamon sticks (optional)

1. Heat water to boiling in medium-size saucepan. Remove from heat. Add tea bags; cover and steep for 5 minutes. Remove tea bags.
2. Stir in honey until dissolved. Add cranberry drink and stir to combine.
3. Serve in small glass cups. To each cup, add a small candy cane or cinnamon stick as a stirrer, if you wish.
Yield: Makes 10 half-cup servings

Mocha Warmer

- 5 cups brewed espresso or strong coffee
- 1/2 cup chocolate syrup
- 1/4 teaspoon mint extract
  Instant whipped cream
  Fresh mint sprigs or grated chocolate, for garnish (optional)
  Small candy canes or cinnamon sticks (optional)

1. Stir together espresso, chocolate syrup, and mint extract in medium-size saucepan. Heat espresso mixture over low heat until warmed through.
2. Pour mixture into small cups or glass mugs. Garnish each serving with whipped cream and, if you wish, a fresh mint sprig or grated chocolate. To each cup, add a candy cane or cinnamon stick as a stirrer, if you wish.
Yield: Makes 10 half-cup servings

Irish Coffee Eggnog Punch

- 2 cartons (1 quart each) eggnog
- 1/3 cup firmly packed light-brown sugar
- 3 tablespoons instant coffee powder
- 1/2 teaspoon ground cinnamon
- 1/2 teaspoon ground nutmeg
- 1 cup Irish whiskey
- 1 quart coffee-flavored ice cream

1. Combine eggnog, brown sugar, coffee powder, cinnamon, and nutmeg in a large bowl.
2. Beat at low speed with an electric mixer until smooth. Stir in Irish whiskey. Chill 1 to 2 hours.
3. Pour into a punch bowl. Top punch with scoops of ice cream.
Yield: Makes 19 half-cup servings

Blackberry Cordial

- 1 cup club soda, chilled
- 2/3 cup crème de cassis
- 1/2 cup raspberry-flavored liqueur
- 1/2 cup blackberry-flavored brandy
  Frozen blackberries, for garnish

1. Combine soda, crème de cassis, liqueur, and brandy in a small bowl.
2. Stir until well blended and store in refrigerator.
3. Serve chilled. Garnish with frozen blackberries.
Yield: Makes 5 half-cup servings

Our distinctive Yuletide drinks include **Irish Coffee Eggnog Punch** (above) *with coffee-flavored ice cream and chilled* **Blackberry Cordial** (right), *a bubbly, berry-flavored apéritif.*

our
merry best
cookies

the delectable dozens on these pages are sure to wow! Make more than you need for friends and parties — baked goodies go fast.

Gingerbread Dough

- 3 cups all-purpose flour
- 1 teaspoon baking soda
- $^1/_2$ teaspoon salt
- 2 teaspoons ground ginger
- 1 teaspoon ground cinnamon
- $^1/_2$ teaspoon grated nutmeg
- $^1/_4$ teaspoon ground cloves
- $^3/_4$ cup firmly packed dark-brown sugar
- $^3/_4$ cup (1$^1/_2$ sticks) unsalted butter, cut into pats
- $^1/_4$ cup unsulfured molasses
- $^1/_4$ cup honey
- 1 egg
  Royal Icing (recipe, this page)
  Assorted food-coloring pastes
  Silver dragées (see Note)

1. In medium bowl, sift together flour, baking soda, salt, ginger, cinnamon, nutmeg, and cloves until blended.
2. In food processor, combine sugar and butter. Whirl until mixture is smooth and creamy, about 1 minute. Add molasses, honey, and egg. Whirl until blended. Add flour mixture. Pulse with on-off motion just until dough clumps together.
3. Scrape dough onto sheet of plastic wrap; press together to form flat disk. Wrap; chill for 2 hours or overnight.
4. Preheat oven to 350°. Lightly grease baking sheets.
5. Roll out dough onto floured surface to $^1/_8$-inch thickness. Cut out cookies using cookie cutters. Place $^1/_2$ inch apart on prepared baking sheets.
6. Bake in preheated 350° oven for 12 to 14 minutes or until cookie edges begin to darken. Cool on baking sheets for a few minutes; transfer cookies to wire racks to cool completely.
7. Make Royal Icing. Reserve about one-quarter for outlining; tint this with food coloring as desired; cover with damp paper towel. Divide remaining icing among custard cups; tint each batch with different coloring, as desired, to "paint" cookies. Thin icings with water, 1 drop at a time, until consistency of sour cream; cover. With small brush, starting at 1 edge of cookie section to be colored, brush on tinted icings in 1 direction. Always work from wet edges, to avoid ridges. Let dry.

Spoon reserved icing for outlining into pastry bag fitted with small writing tip; pipe on.
Yield: Makes about 5 dozen cookies

Gingerbread Wreath:
To make wreath, you'll need fifty 2$^1/_2$-to 3$^1/_2$-inch Holly-Leaf Cookies, six 3-inch Star Cookies, four 3$^1/_2$-inch Ornament Cookies, and two 3-inch Gift-Box Cookies. Place cookies in wreath shape on platter.

Holly-Leaf Cookies:
Cut out holly-leaf cookies using cookie cutters, and berry clusters using small round cutters. Bake as directed. Tint Royal Icing dark green, light green, and red. Frost 1 leaf with dark-green icing. Drizzle on some light-green icing; swirl in, using toothpick or small blunt knife. Repeat with remaining cookies. Pipe tinted red icing onto berry clusters. Let cookies air-dry. Pipe dark-green-icing borders on leaves and red-icing borders on berry clusters. Attach berry clusters to leaves using dollops of icing.

Star, Ornament, and Gift-Box Cookies:
Cut out cookies using cookie cutters. Bake as directed. Frost; decorate with icing and dragées as pictured.
Note: Dragées are not recognized as edible by the Food and Drug Administration. Use for decoration only; remove dragées before eating cookies.

Royal Icing

- 3 tablespoons meringue powder
- 4 cups confectioners' sugar
- 6 tablespoons warm water

1. In medium bowl, combine meringue powder, confectioners' sugar, and water.
2. Beat with an electric mixer 7 to 10 minutes or until icing is stiff.
Yield: Makes 3 cups

Marble-Dipped Chocolate Ribbons

- 2$^1/_4$ cups all-purpose flour
- 2 teaspoons baking powder
- $^1/_2$ teaspoon salt
- $^1/_2$ cup (1 stick) unsalted butter
- 1$^1/_4$ cups firmly packed light-brown sugar
- 1 egg
- 1 tablespoon vanilla
- 3 ounces semisweet chocolate, melted and cooled
- 4 teaspoons solid vegetable shortening
- 6 ounces (6 squares) bittersweet or semisweet chocolate
- 6 ounces (6 squares) white baking chocolate

1. Preheat oven to 375 °. In medium bowl, stir together flour, baking powder, and salt. In large bowl, beat butter and sugar until light and fluffy. Beat in egg and vanilla until blended; beat in melted semisweet chocolate.

Our **Gingerbread Wreath** (opposite) *makes an enchanting edible centerpiece. Bake extra cookies to replenish the wreath as guests nibble away.* **Marble-Dipped Chocolate Ribbons** (above) *feature a swirl of two chocolates.*

2. With mixer on low speed, gradually beat in flour mixture just until combined.

3. Spoon some dough into cookie press fitted with plate for making ribbon strips. Press ribbons, 3 inches long, onto large ungreased baking sheets.

4. Bake in preheated 375° oven for 5 to 7 minutes or until lightly browned. Cool on baking sheets on wire racks for 1 minute. Carefully remove ribbons to wire racks to cool completely. Repeat steps 3 and 4 with remaining dough.

5. In small saucepan over low heat, heat 2 teaspoons shortening and bittersweet chocolate, stirring occasionally, until melted and smooth. Cool to 88° on candy thermometer or until slightly thickened, stirring occasionally, about 20 minutes. Repeat with remaining shortening and white baking chocolate; cool to 84° or until slightly thickened, about 20 minutes.

6. Line cooled baking sheets with aluminum foil.

7. Into medium-size bowl, pour cooled white and bittersweet chocolates next to each other. Carefully swirl knife or thin metal spatula through chocolates to marbleize slightly. Gently dip each cookie straight down into chocolate mixture, then lift straight up; coat 1 or both ends of cookies; let excess chocolate drip off. Place cookies on foil-lined baking sheets. When chocolate is set, gently loosen cookies with thin metal spatula.

Yield: Makes about 8 dozen cookies

*leave Santa a stack of **Double-Chocolate-Chunk Cookies**, packed with candy-coated chocolate pieces, white morsels, and pecans.*

Double-Chocolate-Chunk Cookies

  1 **square (1 ounce) semisweet chocolate**
1 1/4 **cups all-purpose flour**
  1/2 **teaspoon baking soda**
  1/4 **teaspoon salt**
  1/2 **cup (1 stick) unsalted butter**
  1/2 **cup firmly packed light-brown sugar**
  1/2 **cup granulated sugar**
  1 **egg**
  1 **teaspoon vanilla**
  1 **cup mini candy-coated chocolate pieces**
  1/2 **cup white morsels**
  1 **cup chopped pecans**

1. Preheat oven to 375°. Place chocolate in 1-cup measure. Melt in microwave oven.

2. In small bowl, sift together flour, baking soda, and salt until blended.

3. In large bowl, beat butter until creamy; beat in brown and granulated sugars until light and fluffy. Beat in egg and vanilla; beat in melted chocolate.

4. Beat flour mixture into chocolate mixture until well blended. Stir in mini candy-coated chocolate pieces, white morsels, and pecans.

5. Drop tablespoonfuls of dough, 2 inches apart, onto ungreased baking sheets.

6. Bake in preheated 375° oven for 10 to 12 minutes or until slightly browned around edges. Remove from baking sheets to wire racks to cool.

Yield: Makes about 2 dozen cookies

Christmas-Tree Cookies

You can also make these cookies out of Gingerbread Dough, page 85.

  2 **cups all-purpose flour**
  1/4 **teaspoon baking soda**
  1/4 **teaspoon salt**
  1/2 **cup (1 stick) unsalted butter or margarine, softened**
  1/2 **cup sugar**
  1 **tablespoon grated orange rind**
  1 **egg**
  1 **tablespoon orange juice**
      Royal Icing (recipe, page 85)

1. In medium bowl, stir together flour, baking soda, and salt until blended.

2. In large bowl, beat butter, sugar, orange rind, egg, and juice until fluffy. Stir in flour mixture until well blended.

3. Shape dough into two 8-inch disks. Wrap in plastic wrap or waxed paper. Refrigerate until firm enough to handle easily, at least 2 hours.

4. Preheat oven to 375°. Roll out dough onto floured surface to 1/4-inch thickness for unsandwiched cookies or 1/8-inch thickness for sandwiched cookies (see Sandwiched, next page). Cut out cookies using a 3-inch tree-shaped cutter. Place 1 inch apart on greased baking sheets. Repeat, rerolling scraps.

5. Bake in preheated 375° oven for 7 to 8 minutes or until very lightly browned on top. Remove from baking sheets to wire racks to cool.

6. Make Royal Icing. Reserve enough icing for outlining; cover with damp paper towel. Tint remaining icing with food coloring as desired. Thin tinted icing with water, 1 drop at a time, until consistency of sour cream; cover. With a small brush, frost cookies with thinned icing. Decorate, as pictured, using assorted candies and silver dragées (see Note). For snowy trees, dip small crumpled piece of paper towel into reserved white icing, and lightly dab onto trees. Spoon reserved icing for outlining into pastry bag fitted with small writing tip; pipe on cookies as desired.

Sandwiched: Roll out dough to ⅛-inch thickness. Cut into 3-inch tree shapes. Place half of cookies on prepared baking sheet. Cut out centers of remaining cookies with small cutters: For ornaments, make cutouts using a drinking straw or round decorating tip; for trees, use small tree cutter. Bake as directed. Spread plain (uncut) cookie halves with thin layer of seedless raspberry jam or chocolate fudge icing. Sandwich together with remaining cookies, and dust with confectioners' sugar or pipe with Royal Icing.

Note: Silver and gold dragées are not recognized as edible by the Food and Drug Administration. Use for decoration only; remove dragées before eating cookies.

Yield: Makes about 16 cookies

*the possibilities for trimming **Christmas Tree Cookies** are endless! Have fun experimenting — pipe, spread, or dab on icing; dust with powdered sugar; fancy up using the tiniest candies. Or try cutting out a design on one, then sandwiching it along with jam or fudge on another cookie.*

Basic Holiday Cookies

1¼ cups all-purpose flour
½ teaspoon baking powder
¼ teaspoon salt
3 tablespoons unsalted butter
3 tablespoons margarine
½ cup granulated sugar
1 egg
½ teaspoon vanilla

1. In small bowl, stir together flour, baking powder, and salt until blended.
2. In large bowl, beat together butter, margarine, and sugar until creamy. Beat in egg and vanilla until well blended. Stir in flour mixture. Shape into disk; wrap in plastic wrap; refrigerate several hours or overnight.
3. Preheat oven to 350°. Coat baking sheet with nonstick cooking spray.
4. Roll out dough onto lightly floured surface to ³⁄₈-inch thickness. Cut into rounds with 2½-inch cookie cutter. Place 1½ inches apart on prepared baking sheets. Repeat, rerolling scraps.
5. Bake in preheated 350° oven for 10 to 12 minutes or until lightly browned around edges. Remove cookies from baking sheets to wire racks to cool.
Yield: Makes about 2½ dozen cookies

Nut Crescents

Prepare **Basic Holiday Cookie** dough, with the following changes: Substitute ½ teaspoon almond extract for vanilla; reduce flour to 1 cup; stir 1 cup ground blanched almonds or pecans into dough. Wrap in plastic and refrigerate until chilled. For each cookie, roll rounded tablespoon of dough into 3-inch-long rope. Shape into crescent. Place on baking sheets lightly coated with nonstick cooking spray. Bake in preheated 350° oven for 10 to 12 minutes. While still warm, roll in granulated sugar. Cool on wire racks. Decorate with squiggles of white and chocolate icing or melted chocolate. Let harden.
Yield: Makes about 1½ dozen cookies

*add different flavorings to create distinctly delicious variations from one basic cookie recipe. Take a look at some of the options below (clockwise from top right): **Nut Crescents** created with your choice of almonds or pecans; **Apricot Wraps**, which incorporate a subtle orange flavor; refreshing **Double-Mint Drops** dipped in chocolate; and gourmet **Anise Pine-Nut Drops**.*

Piña Colada Drops

Prepare **Basic Holiday Cookie** dough, with the following changes: Substitute 1/2 teaspoon rum extract for vanilla; stir 1/4 cup chopped glacéed pineapple and 1/2 cup shredded coconut into dough. Wrap in plastic and refrigerate until well chilled. For each cookie, drop rounded teaspoon of dough onto baking sheets. Top each cookie with glacéed cherry half. Bake in preheated 350° oven for 10 to 12 minutes. Cool on wire racks.
Yield: Makes about 3 dozen cookies

Apricot Wraps

Prepare **Basic Holiday Cookie** dough, with the following changes: Add 2 teaspoons grated orange rind along with egg to butter mixture. Wrap in plastic and refrigerate until well chilled. Prepare apricot filling: Combine 1/2 cup chopped dried apricots (4 ounces), 1/3 cup orange juice, and 2 tablespoons firmly packed light-brown sugar in small saucepan. Cover; simmer until apricots are very soft, 10 minutes. Purée in food processor. If too thick, add more orange juice; purée. Divide dough into thirds. Roll each third on lightly floured surface into 6-inch square. Cut into 9 squares. Spread scant teaspoon filling on each square, from one corner diagonally across to opposite corner. Fold opposite corners over filling and press to seal. Repeat with remaining dough and filling. Place on baking sheets lightly coated with nonstick cooking spray. Bake in preheated 350° oven 10 to 12 minutes. Cool on wire racks. Sprinkle with confectioners' sugar.
Yield: Makes about 2 dozen cookies

Peanut Butter and Jelly Shortbreads

Prepare **Basic Holiday Cookie** dough, with the following changes: Substitute 1/2 cup smooth peanut butter for margarine. Wrap in plastic and refrigerate until well chilled. Press dough into bottom of 9-inch quiche pan with removable bottom, coated with nonstick cooking spray. With knife, score into 18 pie-shape wedges, without cutting all the way through dough. Bake in preheated 350° oven 10 minutes. Remove from oven. With tip of wooden spoon, press random channels into dough. Fill with grape jelly. Bake 8 minutes more. Remove to wire rack; remove pan side. Cool on wire racks. Cut along score marks into 18 wedges.
Yield: Makes 1 1/2 dozen cookies

Double-Mint Drops

Prepare **Basic Holiday Cookie** dough, with the following changes: Stir 1 1/2 ounces crushed hard peppermint candies (about 3 tablespoons) into dough. Wrap in plastic and refrigerate until well chilled. For each cookie, drop rounded teaspoon of dough onto ungreased baking sheets. Bake in preheated 350° oven for 10 to 12 minutes. Cool on wire racks. Dip half of each cookie into 1/4 cup mint chocolate chips, melted.
Yield: Makes about 4 1/2 dozen cookies

Butterscotch-Pecan Slices

Prepare **Basic Holiday Cookie** dough, with the following changes: Substitute 2/3 cup firmly packed dark-brown sugar for all the granulated sugar; stir 1/2 cup finely chopped pecans into dough. Shape the dough into two 11-inch rolls. Wrap in plastic and refrigerate until well chilled. Cut into 1/4-inch slices. Place on baking sheets. Bake in preheated 350° oven for 10 to 12 minutes. Cool on wire racks.
Yield: Makes about 4 dozen cookies

Anise Pine-Nut Drops

Prepare **Basic Holiday Cookie** dough, with the following changes: Substitute 3/4 teaspoon anise flavoring for vanilla. Wrap in plastic and refrigerate until well chilled. For each cookie, roll 1 rounded teaspoon dough in pine nuts; you'll need about 1/2 cup nuts total. Place on ungreased baking sheets. Bake in preheated 350° oven for 10 to 12 minutes. Cool on wire racks.
Yield: Makes about 2 dozen cookies

*f*or a tropical taste *(from left), substitute rum extract, glacéed pineapple, and shredded coconut to make* **Piña Colada Drops**. *Favorite flavors from childhood are substituted to make yummy* **Peanut Butter and Jelly Shortbreads**, *while brown sugar and chopped nuts are stirred in to create delectable* **Butterscotch-Pecan Slices**.

sweets
for the season

Celebrate the special magic of the holidays with distinctive desserts you make yourself. All these fabulous finales are certain to draw ooh's and aah's, especially the adorable stand-up **Snowman Cake**, made with easy-on-you box mixes and oven-safe bowls. Displayed on a tiered plate stand (opposite), **Chocolate-Orange Cookies** and **Peppermint Cream Puffs** are chic sweets to nibble.

Snowman Cake

2 packages yellow cake mix
  (18.25 ounces each)
2²/₃ cups water
²/₃ cup oil
6 eggs
2 cans (16 ounces each) creamy
  vanilla frosting
1 bag (14 ounces) sweetened
  coconut
  Black food coloring
  Large gum drops, chocolate-
  flavored red and black
  licorice, red fruit leather,
  pretzels

1. Preheat oven to 325°. Position oven rack in center of oven. Grease and flour two 1¹/₂-quart ovenproof glass bowls, two 1-quart ovenproof glass bowls, and one 1¹/₂-cup soufflé dish.
2. Combine mixes, water, oil, and eggs in bowl. Beat on low speed 1 minute, then on medium 3 minutes. Divide into prepared bowls and dish.
3. Bake in preheated 325° oven: 20 to 25 minutes for soufflé dish; 35 to 40 minutes for smaller bowls; 40 to 50 minutes for larger bowls. Cool in bowls on wire rack 10 minutes. Unmold onto rack; cool. (Cakes frost more easily if refrigerated 3 hours or overnight.)
4. Trim rounded tops of bowl cakes to make flat. Invert one larger cake, flat side up, on plate. Spread small amount of frosting in middle. Top with other large cake, flat side down, to form a ball. Spread frosting on top. Place one small cake, flat side up, on top. Spread with frosting; top with other small cake, flat side down, to form a second ball. Push 3 to 4 wooden skewers down center to hold the two round cakes firmly together.
5. Reserve ¹/₂ cup frosting for hat. Frost cake with remaining frosting. Press coconut onto cake. Refrigerate to set, 30 minutes.
6. Cut 5-inch cardboard circle for hat brim. Tint reserved ¹/₂ cup frosting black. Frost brim; place on "head." Place soufflé cake on top for crown; frost. Use skewer to hold hat in place if needed. Refrigerate to set. Decorate as pictured (page 90).
Yield: Makes 24 servings

Chocolate-Orange Cookies

¹/₂ cup semisweet chocolate pieces
1 cup all-purpose flour
³/₄ teaspoon baking powder
¹/₄ teaspoon baking soda
¹/₄ teaspoon salt
¹/₂ cup firmly packed light-brown
  sugar
¹/₄ cup (¹/₂ stick) butter, softened
1 teaspoon grated orange rind
1 egg
  Glaze (recipe follows)

1. Heat chocolate pieces in small heavy saucepan over low heat until melted and smooth. Remove from heat.
2. Combine flour, baking powder, baking soda, and salt in small bowl.
3. Beat together brown sugar, butter, and orange rind with mixer in large bowl until creamy. Beat in egg. Blend in melted chocolate. On low speed, gradually add flour mixture, beating until well blended.
4. Shape dough into ball. Wrap in plastic wrap. Chill about 1 to 1¹/₂ hours or until firm enough to roll.
5. Preheat oven to 350°.
6. Roll out dough onto floured surface to ¹/₄-inch thickness. Cut out cookies using a 2-inch cookie cutter. Place dough on large ungreased baking sheets. Repeat, rerolling scraps.

*top off each sinfully rich slice of **Chocolate Pecan Pie** with a snowdrift of whipped cream crowned with a single pecan. An Italian specialty meaning "half cold," **Christmas Semifreddo** (opposite) enfolds bits of cherries, shortbread, and mint parfait candies.*

7. Bake in preheated 350° oven for 8 to 10 minutes. Remove cookies to wire racks to cool completely.

8. Glaze and decorate as desired with glacéed fruit, colored sugar, or sprinkles.

Glaze: Place 1 cup confectioners' sugar in small bowl. Gradually beat in 1 to 2 tablespoons milk until glaze is thin enough to spread over cooled cookies.

Yield: Makes 2¹/₂ dozen cookies

Peppermint Cream Puffs

For a plain chocolate filling, omit the mint extract and the crushed peppermint candies from the top.

- 1 cup all-purpose flour
- 1 teaspoon sugar
- ¹/₂ teaspoon salt
- 1 cup water
- ¹/₂ cup (1 stick) butter
- 4 eggs
  Mint Cream (recipe follows)
  Chocolate Glaze (optional)
- ¹/₂ cup red and white peppermint candies, crushed

1. Preheat oven to 400°.

2. Mix together flour, sugar, and salt in a small bowl.

3. Bring water and butter to boiling in heavy medium-size saucepan over low heat. Gradually add flour mixture, stirring constantly until mixture is smooth and leaves sides of pan and forms a ball. Remove from heat. Add eggs, one at a time, beating well after each addition.

4. Drop batter by level ¹/₃ cup onto large ungreased baking sheet, spacing 4 inches apart, to make 8 puffs.

5. Bake in lower third of preheated 400° oven for 25 to 30 minutes or until puffed and golden brown.

6. Using a metal pancake turner, gently loosen the puffs from the baking sheet and remove them to a wire rack to cool completely.

7. When the puffs are completely cooled, use a serrated knife to slice off the top quarter of each puff and set aside. Remove any soft dough from inside the puffs and discard. Fill each puff with ¹/₃ cup Mint Cream. Replace the tops of the puffs. Sprinkle the puffs with confectioners' sugar, if you wish.

8. If using glaze, spoon the glaze into a pastry bag fitted with a small writing tip. Pipe the glaze in a drizzle over the top of each puff. Sprinkle the top of each puff with about 1 tablespoon crushed candy.

Mint Cream: Beat together 1 cup heavy cream, ¹/₂ cup sweetened cocoa powder drink mix, and ¹/₂ teaspoon mint extract in small bowl until soft peaks form.

Chocolate Glaze: Heat ¹/₃ cup semisweet chocolate pieces in small heavy saucepan over low heat until melted and smooth.

Yield: Makes 8 servings

Chocolate Pecan Pie

- 1 refrigerated ready-rolled piecrust
- 4 ounces German chocolate
- 1 cup dark corn syrup
- 3 eggs
- ¹/₄ cup firmly packed light-brown sugar
- ¹/₂ teaspoon salt
- 1 teaspoon vanilla
- 1¹/₄ cups pecan halves plus additional whole pecans for garnish
  Sweetened whipped cream

1. Preheat oven to 350°. Roll out piecrust. Fit into 9-inch pie plate; crimp edges decoratively. Refrigerate until ready to use.

2. Melt chocolate in microwave-safe container in microwave oven at full (100%) power for 2 minutes, or in top of double boiler over simmering, not boiling, water.

92

3. Beat together corn syrup, eggs, brown sugar, salt, vanilla, and melted chocolate in bowl until blended. Stir in pecans. Pour mixture into prepared piecrust.

4. Bake in preheated 350° oven for 40 to 45 minutes or until set in center. If crust or top is browning too quickly, tent with aluminum foil during last 15 minutes. Let pie cool completely. Garnish with whipped cream and whole pecans.

Yield: Makes 8 servings

Christmas Semifreddo

¹/₂	cup dried cherries
¹/₄	cup amaretto (almond-flavored liqueur) or kirsch (cherry-flavored liqueur)
¹/₂	cup honey
2	cups heavy cream
¹/₃	cup confectioners' sugar
¹/₂	teaspoon ground cinnamon
¹/₈	teaspoon ground allspice
1	cup chopped shortbread cookies (about 8 cookies)
¹/₂	cup chopped mint parfait thins (14 mints)
	Fresh cherries, raspberries, and strawberries, for garnish
	Fresh mint leaves, for garnish

1. In small saucepan, combine cherries, liqueur, and honey. Bring to simmering. Remove from heat. Let stand until mixture reaches room temperature.

2. Meanwhile, coat 9-inch-diameter 6¹/₂-cup ring mold with nonstick vegetable-oil cooking spray. Line mold with plastic wrap, smoothing out wrinkles.

3. In large bowl, stir together cream, confectioners' sugar, cinnamon, and allspice. Beat mixture just until stiff peaks form.

4. Fold in shortbread cookies, parfait thins, and cherry mixture until blended. Scrape into mold. Freeze for 6 hours or until firm. (Semifreddo can be made ahead and frozen for up to 3 weeks.)

5. To serve, remove mold from freezer; invert onto serving platter. Let stand 5 minutes. Gently tap plate and mold on countertop; slide mold from semifreddo, and remove plastic wrap. Smooth semifreddo with spatula. Garnish with fresh cherries, raspberries, strawberries, and mint leaves.

Yield: Makes 10 servings

*Shape a **Candy-Cane Twist** from sweet dough that's plump with hazelnuts and dried cherries, then drizzle it with icing. Spectacular **Chocolate-Chip Cake** (opposite) is dressed up with chocolate leaves and curls, along with sugar-dusted cranberries.*

Candy-Cane Twist

```
1    package active dry yeast
1/3  cup sugar
1/3  cup warm (105° to 115°) water
1    cup toasted hazelnuts, skinned
       (see Note)
3    cups bread flour OR all-purpose
       flour
1    teaspoon salt
1/4  cup (1/2 stick) unsalted butter, at
       room temperature
1    egg
1/2  cup dried cherries OR golden
       raisins
     Icing (recipe follows)
```

1. Dissolve yeast and 1 teaspoon sugar in warm water. Let stand until foamy, 5 to 10 minutes.
2. Place half of hazelnuts in food processor. Whirl until chopped, then remove and reserve. Place remaining nuts in food processor along with remaining sugar. Whirl until finely ground. Add flour, salt, and butter to processor. With processor running, add egg and the yeast mixture. Whirl until mixture forms ball; whirl 30 seconds more to knead.
3. Transfer dough to large greased bowl;

turn to coat. Cover with damp cloth. Let rise in warm place, away from drafts, until doubled in bulk, about 1 1/2 hours.
4. Punch down dough. On lightly floured surface, knead in remaining nuts and the cherries.
5. Divide dough in half. Roll each half into a 24-inch-long rope. Twist ropes together. On greased baking sheet, form braided loaf into candy-cane shape. Cover with damp cloth. Let dough rise in warm place, away from drafts, until doubled in bulk, about 1 hour.
6. Preheat oven to 350°. Bake for 25 to 30 minutes or until loaf is golden brown and hollow-sounding when tapped with finger. Let loaf cool on wire rack.
7. Prepare Icing. Drizzle or pipe icing over loaf as pictured.
Icing: Stir together 1 1/2 cups confectioners' sugar and about 2 to 3 tablespoons milk until blended and of good icing consistency.
Note: To toast hazelnuts, spread them on baking sheet and bake in preheated 350° oven for 8 to 10 minutes or until toasted. Rub hazelnuts in clean kitchen towel to remove skins.
Yield: Makes 12 servings

Chocolate-Chip Cake

Cake:
```
2 1/2  cups all-purpose flour
   1   tablespoon baking powder
   1   teaspoon salt
 3/4   cup (1 1/2 sticks) unsalted butter,
         at room temperature
   1   cup firmly packed light-brown
         sugar
   1   tablespoon vanilla
   2   eggs
   2   egg whites
 2/3   cup milk
1 1/2  cups semisweet chocolate chips
```

Glaze:
```
   2   teaspoons unsalted butter
   2   teaspoons dark corn syrup
   2   teaspoons water
 3/4   cup semisweet chocolate chips
   3   tablespoons milk
 1/2   teaspoon vanilla
```

Garnish (optional):
```
     Chocolate Curls (recipe follows)
     Chocolate Leaves (recipe follows)
     Sugared Cranberries (recipe follows)
```

1. Preheat oven to 350°. Grease and flour 10-inch (12-cup) fluted tube pan.
2. Combine flour, baking powder, and salt in a medium bowl.
3. Beat butter, sugar, and vanilla in another bowl until smooth and creamy. Add eggs and whites, 1 at a time, beating well after each addition. On low speed, beat in flour mixture alternately with milk. Stir in chips. Spoon in tube pan.
4. Bake in preheated 350° oven for 45 minutes or until wooden pick inserted in center comes out clean. Transfer pan to wire rack to cool 15 minutes. Remove cake from pan and cool on rack.
5. Meanwhile, prepare Glaze: Combine butter, corn syrup, and water in small saucepan. Bring to boiling. Remove from heat. Add chips, stirring constantly, until melted and smooth. Stir in milk and vanilla until well blended.
6. Pour the glaze over the top of cooled cake. Let stand at room temperature until the glaze is set. Garnish with chocolate curls, chocolate leaves, and sugared cranberries, if you wish.
Yield: Makes 12 servings

Chocolate Curls:

1. Melt chocolate by one of the following methods:

Top-of-stove: Place chocolate squares in heavy saucepan over lowest heat or in top of double boiler over simmering water. With wooden spoon or spatula, stir constantly, until chocolate is just melted.

Microwave: Place squares in microwave-safe bowl (do not cover); microwave on high power for 30 seconds. Remove and stir; if only partially melted, repeat microwaving.

2. Pour melted chocolate into foil-lined pan. Refrigerate until hard.

3. Use cheese slicer or vegetable peeler to form curls. Refrigerate.

Chocolate Leaves:

1. See step 1 of Chocolate Curls to melt chocolate.

2. Brush a nontoxic real leaf with coating of melted chocolate. Refrigerate.

3. After chocolate hardens, remove leaf. Refrigerate.

Sugared Cranberries:

1. Melt ¹/₄ cup raspberry or other flavor jam in small saucepan. Add ¹/₂ cup cranberries; stir to coat.

2. When cool enough to handle, roll each in granulated sugar.

95

Strufoli

Strufoli:
- 2 cups all-purpose flour
- 1/4 cup sugar
- 3 eggs
- 1/4 cup vegetable oil
- Grated rind from 1 lemon
- Vegetable oil for frying

Honey Coating:
- 1/2 cup honey
- 1/2 tablespoon sugar
- 1/4 cup candied citron
- 1/4 cup candied lemon peel
- 1/4 cup candied orange peel
- 1/2 teaspoon grated orange rind
- Gilded almonds (see Note) OR nonpareil candies
- Candied cherries

1. Strufoli: Combine flour and sugar in medium bowl. In another bowl, combine eggs, oil, and rind. Stir egg mixture into flour mixture to form soft dough.
2. Turn dough out onto floured surface. Knead until smooth and elastic, about 3 minutes; add more flour as needed to prevent sticking. Shape dough into 3/4-inch-thick disk. With knife, slice piece of dough about 1/2 inch wide. On lightly floured surface, roll into 1/2-inch-thick rope. Cut rope into 1/2-inch pieces. Repeat with remaining dough.
3. In large skillet, heat 1/2 inch vegetable oil until it registers 375° on deep-fat-frying thermometer. Add enough strufoli to fill skillet; cook until golden brown, stirring frequently. With slotted spoon, remove to paper towels to drain. Repeat with remaining strufoli.
4. Coating: In heavy large saucepan over medium heat, heat honey and sugar until mixture registers 265° on candy thermometer. Remove from heat. Stir in citron, lemon peel, orange peel, and rind. Stir in strufoli until well coated. When mixture is cool enough, with wet hands, arrange strufoli on platter in shape of ring or mound. Sprinkle with gilded almonds or nonpareils and cherries.

Note: Gilded almonds are not recognized by the Food and Drug Administration as edible; use for decoration only.

Yield: Makes about 10 servings

Strufoli (top), *a star on the Italian holiday table, is rolled in a citrusy honey glaze and capped with candied cherries and gilded almonds.* **Apple Christmas Tree Tart**, *decked with frosted berries, boasts fresh fruit slices brushed with apricot preserves. "Tie" a fondant ribbon on chocolate-frosted* **Gift-Box Cannoli Cake** *(opposite), which features layers of creamy ricotta and chocolate-chip filling.*

Apple Christmas Tree Tart

- 1/3 cup apricot preserves
- 1 package (11 ounces) piecrust mix
- 1/3 cup plus 1 tablespoon sugar
- 1 1/2 to 2 Golden Delicious apples, peeled, cored, and thinly sliced (3 cups)
- 1 teaspoon fresh lemon juice
- Frosted Berries, for garnish (optional; recipe follows)

1. Preheat oven to 400°. Lightly flour large baking sheet.
2. Press preserves through fine-mesh sieve into small saucepan; cover and set aside.
3. Prepare piecrust mix for 2-crust pie, using 1/3 cup sugar, following package directions.
4. On lightly floured surface, shape piecrust dough into a block. Roll dough out into 12 x 11-inch rectangle. Roll up dough on rolling pin; unroll onto baking sheet.
5. Starting at center of top of rectangle, using tip of small paring knife, lightly outline dough into shape of Christmas tree with trunk, making 3 branch indentations, about 1-inch deep on each side of tree. Cut out; reserve trimmings. On a floured surface, use about one-quarter of the trimmings to roll into a 22-inch rope. Place rope on one side of tree, following outer edge of tree. Repeat with another quarter of trimmings; attach to other side of tree. Pinch edge of tree together with rope to adhere; with fingers, flute as for piecrust.
6. Gather remaining trimmings. On lightly floured surface, roll out dough. Cut out star with 2 3/8-inch cookie cutter. Cover star with dampened paper towel.
7. Toss apples with lemon juice in bowl. Arrange over tree, overlapping slightly to fill in.
8. Heat preserves just until hot and bubbly. Brush apple slices and star, using half the preserves. Place star on sheet. Sprinkle apple with remaining 1 tablespoon sugar.
9. Bake tart and star in preheated 400° oven for 20 to 25 minutes or until crust is golden and apples are tender. Remove star when golden. If parts of crust brown too quickly, cover with pieces of foil.

10. Brush underside of star with apricot preserves for "glue." Place star on top of tree.

11. Brush apples with remaining preserves. Cool. Garnish with Frosted Berries, if desired.

Frosted Berries: Brush berries, such as cranberries, blueberries, and/or cherries, with maple syrup. Roll in granulated sugar. Place on waxed paper to dry.

Yield: Makes 8 servings

Gift-Box Cannoli Cake

Chocolate Frosting and Glaze:
- 1 cup heavy cream plus additional for thinning, if needed
- 8 squares (1 ounces each) semisweet chocolate, chopped

Simple Syrup:
- 1/4 cup water
- 1/4 cup orange juice
- 1/2 cup granulated sugar

Cake:
- 8 eggs, separated
- 2/3 cup granulated sugar
- 1 1/4 teaspoons vanilla
- 2/3 cup all-purpose flour

Cannoli Filling:
- 2 containers (15 ounces each) ricotta cheese
- 3/4 cup confectioners' sugar
- 2 teaspoons vanilla
- 2 tablespoons grated orange rind
- 3/4 cup mini semisweet-chocolate chips OR 1/2 cup mini semisweet-chocolate chips plus 1/4 cup chopped glacéed-fruit mix

Decorations:
- 1/3 cup ready-to-use rolled white fondant (see Note)
  Red and green decorating icing (not gel) OR small red and green candies (optional)
  Cornstarch, for dusting

1. Prepare Chocolate Frosting and Glaze: Bring cream to boiling in saucepan over medium-high heat. Remove from heat. Stir in chocolate until melted and smooth. Pour half into small bowl;

refrigerate until frosting hardens to good spreading consistency, about 2 hours. Cover remaining half of chocolate mixture; let stand at room temperature to use as glaze.

2. Simple Syrup: Heat water, juice, and granulated sugar to boiling in saucepan; boil 1 minute. Refrigerate until ready to use.

3. Prepare Cake: Preheat oven to 350°. Grease two 8 x 8 x 2-inch square metal baking pans. Line bottoms with waxed paper; grease paper.

4. Beat egg whites in large bowl at medium speed until stiff peaks form. Working quickly and using same beaters, beat yolks, sugar, and vanilla in another large bowl with electric mixer until very thick and lemon-colored, about 2 minutes. At low speed, beat in flour until just blended. Spoon 1/4 cup whites into yolk mixture to lighten. Fold in remaining whites until just blended; do not over-mix. Pour into pans.

5. Bake in preheated 350° oven until center of each cake springs back when touched lightly with finger, about 15 minutes. Cool cakes in pans on wire rack for 10 minutes. Remove cakes from pans; cool completely on wire rack, about 30 minutes. Cakes will deflate slightly while cooling. With long serrated knife, gently cut each cake horizontally in half to make total of 4 layers.

*a year-round classic, **New York-Style Cheesecake** can be dressed up for the holidays. Try topping it with fruit slices, toffee crunch, ripe raspberries, whipped-cream mounds, coffee beans and chocolate shavings, piped icing, gilded almonds, or fresh mint and sugar-glazed cranberries.*

6. Prepare Cannoli Filling: Beat ricotta, confectioners' sugar, and vanilla in large bowl at high speed until blended and smooth. Stir in rind, chocolate chips, and glacéed-fruit mix, if using.

7. Assemble Cake: Set cooling rack into large tray. Cut 8 x 8-inch piece of cardboard; wrap in plastic wrap. Place a cake layer, cut side up, on cardboard on rack. Brush layer with ¼ of syrup; top with ⅓ of filling. Repeat twice more with cake, syrup, and filling, ending with last cake layer, cut side down. Brush remaining syrup over top of cake. Smooth out filling between layers. Spread cooled frosting over sides and top of cake to seal in filling. Refrigerate 1 hour to harden frosting.

8. Pour room-temperature glaze over top. Glaze should be thick but pourable; if too thick, very gently fold in 1 to 2 tablespoons heavy cream, without creating bubbles. Smooth glaze carefully with long metal spatula to coat top and sides of cake. Refrigerate 1 hour, until glaze is firm.

9. Meanwhile, prepare fondant ribbons: Lightly dust work surface and rolling pin with cornstarch. Roll fondant into six 13 x 1-inch strips. Place 1 strip across width of cake and down sides, 1½ inches from end of cake. Place another strip across length of cake and down sides, 2 inches from end of cake. Cut two 3-inch strips fondant, with notched ends; attach where fondant-ribbons intersect, for bow ties. Cut remaining 4 strips into 3½-inch lengths; fold in half, arrange in bow shape and place in center where ribbons cross. If you wish, pipe red-and-green-dotted pattern on ribbons or attach red and green candies. Refrigerate overnight.

Note: Fondant and other cake-decorating products are sold in specialty cake stores.

Yield: Makes 16 servings

New York-Style Cheesecake

Crumb Crust:

- 1½ cups graham-cracker crumbs
- ¼ cup sugar
- ½ cup unsalted butter, melted

Cheesecake:

- 3 packages (8 ounces each) cream cheese, at room temperature
- 1¼ cups sugar
- 4 eggs
- 2 teaspoons vanilla
- 2 teaspoons fresh lemon juice

Topping:

- 1 container (16 ounces) sour cream
- ¼ cup sugar
- 1 teaspoon vanilla

1. Preheat oven to 350°.

2. Prepare Crumb Crust: Combine graham-cracker crumbs, sugar, and butter in bowl. Scrape into 9-inch springform pan; press evenly over bottom and 1 inch up sides of pan.

3. Prepare Cheesecake: Beat cream cheese and sugar at medium speed in large bowl until blended. Beat in eggs, vanilla, and juice until blended. Pour into prepared pan.

4. Bake in preheated 350° oven for 50 minutes or until puffed and golden. Transfer to wire rack; let stand 15 minutes. Increase oven temperature to 450°.

5. Prepare Topping: Stir together sour cream, sugar, and vanilla in small bowl until blended. Spoon over top of cheesecake, spreading evenly.

6. Bake 10 minutes, just until topping is set. Transfer cheesecake to rack to cool completely. Refrigerate overnight. Remove sides of pan; slice cake into wedges. Garnish slices as you wish (see Cheesecake Garnishes).

Yield: Makes 16 servings

Cheesecake Garnishes

Fruit Slices
Arrange thinly sliced orange or other fruit slices on top.

Toffee Crunch
Coarsely chop toffee candy bars and walnuts to sprinkle.

Ripe Raspberries
Arrange fresh raspberries on slices; drizzle with melted white chocolate.

Whipped-Cream Mounds
Pipe whipped cream from pastry bag with small star tip; using tweezers, arrange silver dragées (see Note) on tip of each star.

Coffee Beans and Chocolate Shavings
Pipe large rosette of whipped cream on each slice; dust lightly with cocoa powder. Arrange chocolate-covered espresso beans and shaved chocolate on top.

Piped Icing
In separate bowls, mix white and chocolate confectioners' sugars with water until thin frosting consistency. Pipe each from pastry bag fitted with small writing tip.

Gilded Almonds
Decorate with gilded almonds and gold and silver dragées (see Note).

Mint and Sugar-Glazed Cranberries
Drizzle melted chocolate on each slice. Add dragées (see Note), a mint sprig, sugared cranberries (see Sugared Fruits recipe), and a chocolate twig.

Sugared Fruits
Beat together 2 tablespoons powdered egg whites and 2 tablespoons water until blended and frothy. Brush lightly on assorted fruits (such as strawberries, cranberries, grapes, kumquats, and lady apples). Sprinkle sugar over fruits, coating evenly. Place on waxed paper to air-dry.

Note: Dragées and gilded almonds are not recognized by the Food and Drug Administration as edible; use for decoration only.

a joyful feast

Menu

amid the gaiety and excitement of the Christmas season, our hearts are warmed by friends and family who gather for an evening of festive fare. Laughter and cheer abound as guests are welcomed inside by the spicy aromas wafting from the kitchen. **Peppered Rib Roast** (opposite) is deliciously accompanied by **Thyme Roasted Potatoes** and **Green Beans with Roasted Hazelnuts**. For an elegant prelude to the joyful feast, begin with **Marinated Skewered Shrimp** and **Tapenade Toasts** (below).

Marinated Skewered Shrimp

- ¹/₂ cup bottled Italian salad dressing
- ¹/₄ cup chopped fresh dill
- ¹/₈ to ¹/₄ teaspoon ground hot red pepper
- 1 pound fresh shrimp, shelled and deveined (about 30 shrimp)
- 15 large snow peas
- 30 wooden (4-inch) skewers

1. Combine dressing, dill, hot red pepper, and shrimp in plastic food-storage bag. Push out all air, seal, and marinate in refrigerator up to 2 hours.
2. Meanwhile, bring a large skillet of water to simmering. Add snow peas; cook 1 minute. Drain; rinse under cold water. Split pea pods apart.
3. Drain shrimp; place marinade in large skillet. Bring to simmering. Add shrimp in single layer; cook over low heat until opaque, about 3 minutes, turning over halfway during cooking. Drain; refrigerate up to 2 days.
4. To serve, wrap snow pea half around each shrimp, attaching overlap with skewer.

Yield: Makes 30 skewers

Continue the merry mood with **Mushroom and Brie Tartlets** *(below), sumptuous hors d'oeuvres presented in flaky pastry shells. Warming* **Butternut-Leek Bisque** *is laced with apple and sage. Traditional* **Caesar Salad with Crispy Croutons** *(opposite) boasts the distinctive tastes of anchovies and Dijon-style mustard.*

Tapenade Toasts

16 slices (¹/₂-inch) French bread
    Olive-oil cooking spray OR
    1 tablespoon olive oil
 1 clove garlic
¹/₄ cup pitted oil-cured black olives
 1 cup very low-sodium pinto beans,
    rinsed and drained
 2 teaspoons lemon juice
 1 teaspoon capers
³/₄ teaspoon sugar
    Cherry tomatoes, for garnish
    Parsley leaves, for garnish

1. Preheat oven to 300°. Arrange the bread in a single layer on the baking sheet. Coat the bread with the olive-oil cooking spray, or brush lightly with the olive oil.
2. Bake in preheated 300° oven for 15 minutes or until crisped and lightly golden. (Can be made up to 1 week in advance; cool completely and store airtight at room temperature.)
3. To prepare the tapenade, place the garlic in a food processor. Whirl until finely chopped. Add olives, beans, lemon juice, capers, and sugar. Whirl until the mixture is smooth and blended, scraping down the work bowl as needed. Refrigerate the tapenade, covered, for up to 1 week.
4. To serve, spread tapenade on toasts. Cut tomatoes into wedges. Garnish each toast with tomato wedge and parsley leaf. Serve at room temperature.
Yield: Makes 16 servings

Mushroom and Brie Tartlets

Tart Shells:
1¹/₂ cups all-purpose flour
 2 tablespoons buttermilk powder
    OR dry milk powder
¹/₄ teaspoon salt
 6 tablespoons (³/₄ stick) cold butter,
    cut into pats
¹/₃ cup cold water

Tart Filling:
¹/₂ pound white button mushrooms
¹/₂ pound wild mushrooms, such as
    cremini or oyster OR white
    button mushrooms
 2 tablespoons olive oil
 3 green onions, chopped
¹/₄ cup pale dry sherry
 1 tablespoon balsamic vinegar
³/₄ teaspoon salt
 6 ounces brie cheese, end rind
    removed

1. Prepare Tart Shells: Combine flour, buttermilk powder, salt, and butter in food processor. Pulse with on-off motion until mixture resembles coarse meal. Add water. Whirl until mixture begins to clump together. Shape dough into ball and flatten into 6-inch disk on lightly floured board. Wrap in plastic wrap and refrigerate at least 1 hour or up to 4 days.
2. Preheat oven to 300°.
3. Roll dough to ³/₈-inch thickness on floured board; cut into eight 5-inch circles, OR roll dough into 8-inch log; cut into eight 1-inch-thick pieces. Roll each piece into 5-inch circle. Fit into eight 4-inch individual tart pans; roll edges in toward center and press against side to seal. (If tartlet pans are unavailable, shape circles on a baking sheet. Roll a ³/₄-inch edge and flute.) Pierce tartlets with fork and place on baking sheet.
4. Bake in preheated 300° oven for 25 to 30 minutes or until golden. Cool completely on racks. Store airtight at room temperature for up to 2 weeks.
5. Prepare Tart Filling: Slice mushrooms. Heat 1 tablespoon oil in large skillet over medium-high heat. Add half the mushrooms; cook, stirring occasionally, 5 to 7 minutes or until golden. Remove mushrooms to a plate. Repeat with remaining oil and mushrooms.

6. Combine the green onions, sherry, vinegar, and salt in skillet. Cook until mixture is reduced to a syrupy consistency. Remove from heat. Add mushrooms and toss to combine. (Can be made up to 1 day ahead and refrigerated, covered.)

7. To serve: Preheat oven to 350°. Cut brie into thin slices. Divide among tart shells, arranging slices and trimming to fit. Divide mushroom mixture among tartlets (about ¼ cup per tartlet), mounding on top.

8. Bake in preheated 350° oven for 8 minutes or just until heated through and cheese is melted. Serve warm.

Yield: Makes 8 servings

Butternut-Leek Bisque

 2 large leeks
 2 teaspoons olive oil
 1 large butternut squash (about 2 pounds), seeded, peeled, and cubed
 1 small apple, peeled, cored, and cubed
 2 cups water
 1 can (13¾ ounces) reduced-sodium chicken broth
 1½ teaspoons salt
 ¼ teaspoon ground sage
 ¼ teaspoon ground white pepper
 ⅛ teaspoon ground allspice
 ¾ cup half-and-half OR milk
 Fresh chives, for garnish (optional)

1. Trim leeks, leaving 2 inches of green. Chop leeks; rinse thoroughly in water to remove any grit; drain.

2. Heat oil in large saucepan over medium heat. Add leeks; cover and cook 8 minutes, stirring occasionally. Add squash, apple, water, broth, salt, sage, pepper, and allspice. Bring to simmering; cook 20 minutes or until vegetables are soft. Working in batches, place vegetable mixture and liquid in blender or food processor. Whirl until smooth. (Can be made up to 4 days ahead and refrigerated, covered.)

3. To serve, bring leek mixture to simmering in saucepan. Stir in half-and-half; gently heat through. Garnish with fresh chives, if you wish.

Yield: Makes 8 servings

Caesar Salad with Crispy Croutons

Dressing:
 2 canned anchovy fillets
 3 tablespoons fresh lemon juice
 1 teaspoon Dijon-style mustard
 1 tablespoon no-cholesterol, fat-free liquid egg substitute (optional)
 ½ small clove garlic
 ½ to ¾ teaspoon salt
 ¼ teaspoon ground white pepper
 ½ cup olive oil

Salad:
 1 head (1 pound) romaine lettuce, torn into pieces
 ¼ cup grated Parmesan cheese
 Crispy Croutons (recipe follows)

1. Prepare Dressing: Combine anchovy, lemon juice, mustard, egg substitute if using, garlic, salt, and pepper in blender. With blender running, add oil in thin stream, blending until thick and creamy. Store, refrigerated, for up to 7 days.

2. Prepare Salad: Toss together romaine, Parmesan, and ½ cup of the dressing in salad bowl. Garnish with croutons and serve.

Yield: Makes 8 servings

Crispy Croutons: Cut 4 ounces French bread into 1-inch cubes. Arrange in single layer on baking sheet and lightly coat with olive-oil cooking spray. Bake in preheated 325° oven for 15 minutes or until golden. Toss in bowl with 1 tablespoon grated Parmesan cheese. Cool completely and store airtight at room temperature for up to 10 days.

Peppered Rib Roast

 1 standing beef rib roast, small end (about 7 pounds)
 4 teaspoons cracked pepper
 1 teaspoon kosher (coarse) salt OR ¾ teaspoon table salt
 Fresh thyme sprigs (optional)

1. Have butcher remove chine bone and feather bones from meat, and trim off excess fat.

2. Preheat oven to 325°.

3. Place meat in roasting pan. Sprinkle with pepper and salt.

4. Roast in preheated 325° oven for the following doneness:

Rare — 25 minutes per pound or about 3 hours (internal temperature on meat thermometer is 140°).

Medium — 30 minutes per pound or about 3½ hours (internal temperature on meat thermometer is 160°).

Well — 35 minutes per pound or about 4 hours (internal temperature on meat thermometer is 170°).

5. Let meat stand at least 30 minutes before slicing.

Yield: Makes 12 generous servings

Thyme Roasted Potatoes

 2 pounds small new potatoes, halved
 1½ tablespoons olive oil
 ½ teaspoon salt
 ¼ teaspoon black pepper
 2 tablespoons fresh thyme leaves

1. Preheat oven to 325°.

2. Toss together potatoes, oil, salt, and pepper in 13 x 9 x 2-inch baking pan until potatoes are coated.

3. Bake in preheated 325° oven for 30 minutes.

4. Toss in thyme leaves and bake 45 minutes more or until potatoes are fork-tender.

Yield: Makes 10 servings

Green Beans with Roasted Hazelnuts

1½ pounds green beans, trimmed
2 tablespoons unsalted butter
½ teaspoon salt
⅓ cup toasted hazelnuts, chopped
   (see Note)

1. Bring large pot of water to boiling. Add beans; cook, uncovered, 8 to 10 minutes or until tender-crisp. Drain.
2. Heat butter in pot until golden brown and fragrant, about 3 minutes. Add beans and salt, tossing to coat. Place in serving dish; sprinkle with chopped hazelnuts.
Note: To toast hazelnuts, place nuts on baking sheet in preheated 350° oven. Bake, stirring occasionally, until toasted, about 10 minutes. Rub the hazelnuts in cotton dish towel to remove the skins.
Yield: Makes 8 servings

Fennel and Red Pepper Gratin

2 large fennel bulbs (about
   1¼ pounds)
2 sweet red peppers
1 cup orange juice
½ cup white wine OR chicken broth
2 cloves garlic, smashed
½ teaspoon dried leaf basil, crumbled
¼ teaspoon fennel seeds, crushed
⅛ to ¼ teaspoon crushed red pepper
   flakes
½ teaspoon salt
1 slice fresh bread
1 tablespoon cold unsalted butter,
   cut into pieces
2 tablespoons grated Parmesan
   cheese
   Chopped fennel fronds (see Note),
   for garnish (optional)

1. Cut fennel bulbs into thin wedges, slicing through the core to keep wedges intact. Cut red peppers into 4 x 1-inch pieces.
2. Combine orange juice, wine, garlic, basil, fennel, red pepper flakes, and salt in large skillet. Add fennel in single layer. Bring to simmering; cover and cook 6 minutes. Add sweet red peppers; cover and cook 8 minutes more. Remove with slotted spoon and arrange in 13 x 9 x 2-inch baking dish.
3. Boil cooking liquids until reduced to ⅓ cup. Pour over fennel mixture. (Can be prepared up to 3 days ahead, covered, and refrigerated.)
4. Preheat oven to 325°.
5. Combine bread, butter, and 1 tablespoon of the Parmesan in food processor. Whirl until crumbed. Sprinkle over gratin; sprinkle with remaining Parmesan.
6. Bake in preheated 325° oven for 25 minutes or until golden and heated through. Serve hot or warm. Garnish with chopped fennel fronds, if you wish.
Note: Fennel fronds are the feathery part of the stalk. They resemble fresh dill sprigs.
Yield: Makes 12 servings

*f**ennel and Red Pepper Gratin** (below) is a colorful holiday dish that's brimming with robust flavor. Too rich to resist, our **Brownie and Raspberry Bavarian** (opposite) is made with layers of rich chocolate, a jelled berry blend, and creamy topping.*

Brownie and Raspberry Bavarian

You have three choices of pans to use for this dessert: a curved scalloped-bottom nut bread pan, a 1-pound coffee can, or a 4- to 5-cup loaf pan. Leftover brownie can be served for another dessert.

Brownie:
1 package (12 ounces) semisweet
   chocolate pieces
2 cups all-purpose flour
1½ teaspoons baking powder
½ teaspoon salt
½ cup (1 stick) butter or margarine,
   softened
1 cup firmly packed light-brown
   sugar
1 tablespoon vanilla
2 eggs
2 egg whites

Raspberry Bavarian:
- 2 packages (10 ounces each) frozen raspberries in syrup, thawed
- 2 envelopes unflavored gelatin
- 1/2 cup cranberry juice
- 1/2 cup sugar
- 1 tablespoon lemon juice
- 3/4 cup heavy cream, whipped

Decoration:
- 1 cup heavy cream
- 2 tablespoons confectioners' sugar
- Fresh or frozen dry-pack raspberries and blackberries, for garnish (optional)
- Fresh mint leaves, for garnish (optional)

1. Preheat oven to 350°. Line 13 x 9 x 2-inch baking pan with aluminum foil. Coat with nonstick vegetable-oil cooking spray.

2. To prepare Brownie: Heat chocolate pieces in small heavy saucepan over low heat until melted and smooth.

3. Combine flour, baking powder, and salt in small bowl.

4. Beat together butter, brown sugar, and vanilla in large bowl until creamy and smooth. Add eggs, one at a time, and egg whites, beating well after each addition. On slow speed, gradually beat in flour mixture until well blended. Blend in melted chocolate. Spread evenly in prepared pan.

5. Bake in preheated 350° oven for 35 minutes or until wooden pick inserted in center comes out clean. Remove brownie to wire rack to cool.

6. To prepare Raspberry Bavarian: Place raspberries in food processor or blender. Whirl at high speed until puréed. Pour in fine-mesh wire sieve set over large bowl; press seeds with rubber spatula to extract all juice; discard seeds.

7. Combine gelatin and cranberry juice in small heavy saucepan; let gelatin soften for about 5 minutes. Add sugar. Place over low heat, stirring occasionally, for 10 to 15 minutes or until gelatin and sugar are completely dissolved. Cool.

8. Stir gelatin mixture and lemon juice into puréed raspberries. Place raspberry mixture over bowl of ice water; whisk constantly until mixture is thickened and mounds slightly when dropped from

spoon. Fold in whipped cream until no streaks of white remain. Pour mixture into 4- to 5-cup nut bread pan or loaf pan, or 1-pound coffee can. (If nut bread pan is lined with tin, place a layer of plastic wrap inside the pan, making sure to cover inside completely. Follow same procedure for coffee can.) There will be about 1/2 cup mixture left over; pour into small custard cup and chill for a snack. Refrigerate 3 to 4 hours or until firm.

9. To assemble: Measure bottom of nut loaf pan or loaf pan, and cut out a section of brownie the same size. If using coffee can, measure diameter and length of coffee can and cut out 2 rectangular sections of brownie the same size.

10. Run small metal spatula around sides of nut loaf pan or regular loaf pan to loosen Raspberry Bavarian. Center

brownie on top of Bavarian; invert mold onto brownie. Trim off any brownie not covered by raspberry mold. If using coffee can, invert open end of can onto 1 end of sheet of waxed paper-lined baking sheet. Using a can opener, open other end of can; remove lid and carefully slide mold onto baking sheet. Slice mold lengthwise in half. Using a pancake turner, slide half of Bavarian mold, flat side down, onto 1 brownie section. Repeat with other brownie and Bavarian; place end-to-end on large serving platter.

11. To decorate: Beat heavy cream with confectioners' sugar in a small bowl until soft peaks form. Frost Bavarian with the whipped cream. Decorate with berries and mint leaves, if desired.

Yield: Makes 12 servings

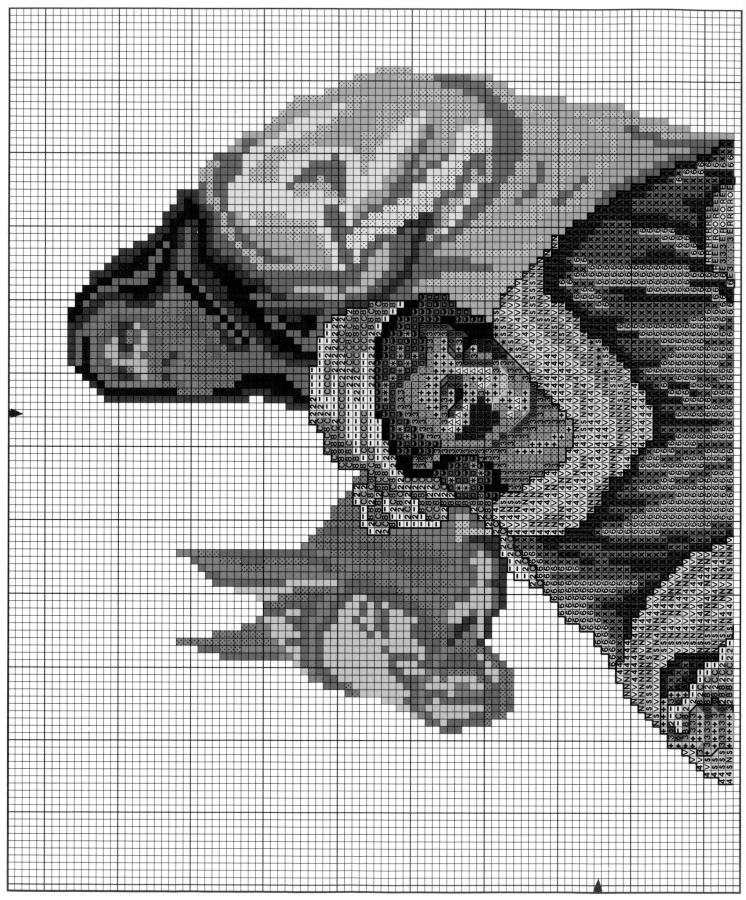

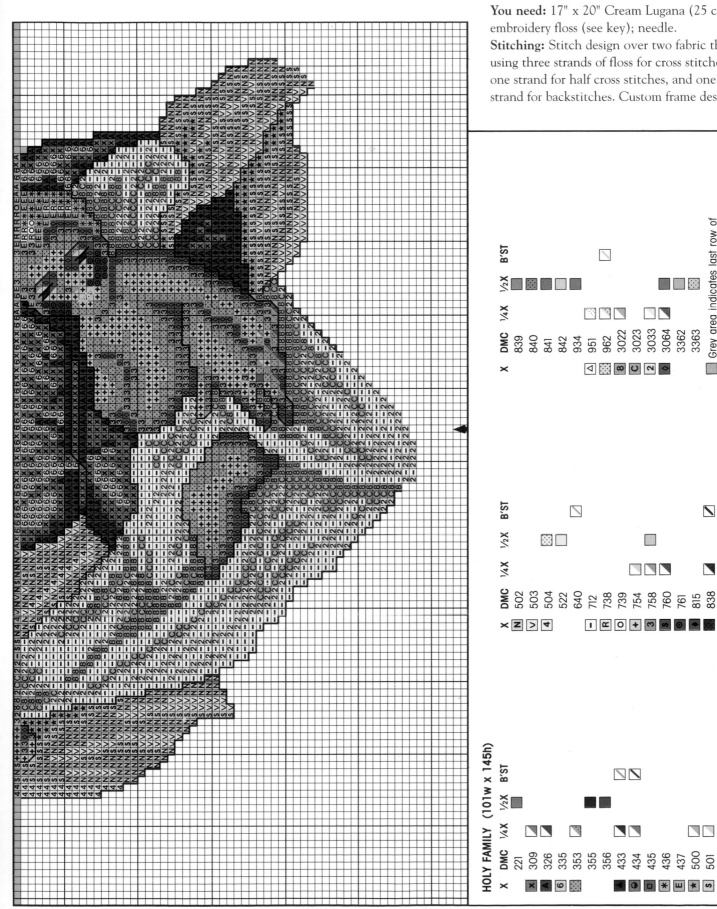

Holy Family

You need: 17" x 20" Cream Lugana (25 ct); embroidery floss (see key); needle.

Stitching: Stitch design over two fabric threads using three strands of floss for cross stitches, one strand for half cross stitches, and one strand for backstitches. Custom frame design.

X	DMC	¼X	½X	B'ST
	839			
	840			
	841			
	842			
	934			
	951			
	962			
⊲	3022			
8	3023			
C	3033			
2	3064			
◇	3362			
	3363			

Grey area indicates last row of top section of design.

X	DMC	¼X	½X	B'ST
N	502			
V	503			
◢	504			
	522			
	640			
I	712			
R	738			
O	739			
+	754			
3	758			
S	760			
●	761			
◆	815			
■	838			

HOLY FAMILY (101w x 145h)

X	DMC	¼X	½X	B'ST
✕	221			
◢	309			
6	326			
◢	335			
	353			
◢	355			
◐	356			
□	433			
✱	434			
E	435			
★	436			
S	437			
	500			
	501			

Gingerbread Nativity

You need: Gingerbread Dough (page 85); meringue powder; confectioners' sugar; paring knife; lightweight cardboard; pastry bag; medium writing tip; wire racks.

Making patterns: Cut full-size patterns from cardboard.

Cutting shapes: Roll chilled dough to ⅛" thickness. Cut the following shapes: *Mary, Joseph, and manger* – Use patterns. *Bases* – 1" x 3½" for Mary, 1" x 3" for Joseph, and 1" x 1¾" for manger. *Stable* – two 2" x 6" pieces for roof, two 2" x 6½" pieces for sides, and one 7½" x 6½" piece for back.

Baking: Bake as directed in recipe. Cool on wire racks.

Preparing icing: In medium bowl, combine 1 tablespoon meringue powder, 1⅓ cups confectioners' sugar, and 2 tablespoons warm water. Beat with an electric mixer 7 to 10 minutes or until icing is stiff. Spoon icing into pastry bag fitted with medium writing tip.

Decorating: Pipe icing onto one side of stable back to resemble boards. Refer to grey lines on patterns to pipe icing onto Mary, Joseph, and manger pieces. Let dry thoroughly.

Assembling: Use icing to assemble stable and to attach bases, holding pieces in place until icing starts to set. Lay stable flat and prop remaining pieces until icing dries thoroughly.

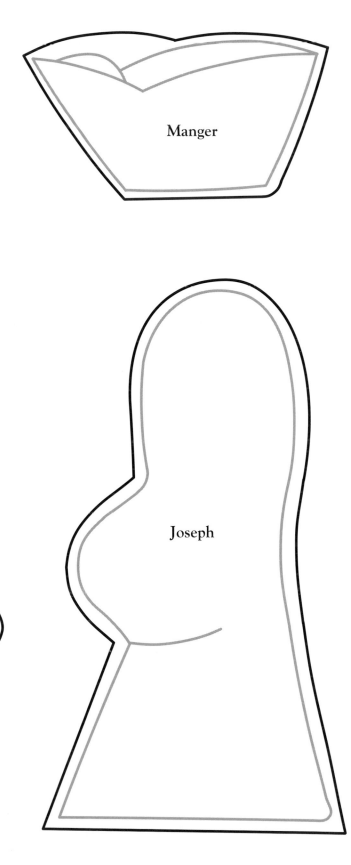

Manger

Mary

Joseph

Quilted Crèche Wall Hanging

Finished size: 17" x 20½"

You need: Fabric – ½ yd blue star print; ½ yd muslin; ¼ yd each 2 coordinating red checks; ⅛ yd green check; 12" squares of blue denim, beige gingham, blue gingham; scraps – burlap, white fleece, solid yellow, solid brown, 5 different yellow prints, 2 red ginghams, 2 blue prints, blue stripe; 19" x 22" piece of batting; paper-backed fusible web; 5 wood buttons; embroidery floss – black, white, yellow, red; ecru pearl cotton; red ribbon; safety pins.

Cutting patchwork: *Blue gingham* – Cut piece 9½" x 10". *Green check* – Cut piece 3¼" x 9½". *Red checks* – From one, cut two strips 1½" x 12¼"; from other, cut two strips 1½" x 11¼". *Stars* – Cut two border strips 3½" x 14½" and two strips 3½" x 17½". Cut binding strips (not on bias), two 2" x 17½", two 2" x 20½". *Muslin backing* – Cut piece 17" x 20½".

Cutting appliqués: Fuse web to remaining fabric. Use full-size patterns (pages 110-112) to cut the following: *Blue denim* – Cut barn sides/roof. *Beige gingham* – Use outline of barn sides/roof pattern to cut barn "interior." *Solid yellow* – Cut manger star and Child's halo. *Yellow prints* – Cut stars A-E, two halos (for Mary and Joseph). *Solid brown* – Cut manger. *Burlap* – Cut blanket. *Red gingham* – Cut two figures. *Blue prints* – Cut one each headdress. *Muslin* – Cut faces. *Fleece* – Cut two sheep (trace one; flip pattern; trace second). *Blue stripe* – Cut two donkeys (trace one; flip pattern; trace second).

Stitching patchwork: *Pin; stitch pieces together, right sides facing; ¼" seams allowed.* Stitch blue gingham to green check. Stitch red check strips to sides of assembly, then stitch strips to ends. Stitch star borders to sides, then each end.

Appliquéing: Following the photo, fuse barn interior to blue gingham along blue/green seam. Fuse denim sides/roof to interior. Position Mary at left and Joseph at right; pin. Position Child (manger, halo, head, and blanket) between Mary and Joseph; add manger star above Child; pin; fuse all pieces in place. Pin stars A-E across blue gingham sky; fuse. Pin donkeys and sheep on green-check grass; fuse.

Details: Embroider overcast stitches on figures and animals. *Sheep* – With black floss, embroider ears. *Donkey tails* – Thread needle with ecru pearl cotton. Push needle down through fabric at rump, then back up, leaving long strands at front. Separate strands and divide them in three bunches; braid a 1"L tail; knot ends; trim evenly. *Child's halo and stars* – Add radiating lines to halo and to manger star with yellow. Sew a button to each star in the sky.

Assembling: Stack muslin backing, batting, and appliquéd top (face up); pin; baste a large "X" across assembly, then baste around sides. Machine-stitch around patch pieces.

Finishing: Trim batting even with quilt top and backing. Pin binding to quilt top, right sides facing, edges even, turning corners smoothly. Stitch seam (¼"). Bring binding to back of quilt, and fold under raw edge; slipstitch in place. To make hanger, sew ends of red ribbon to top back corners of wall hanging.

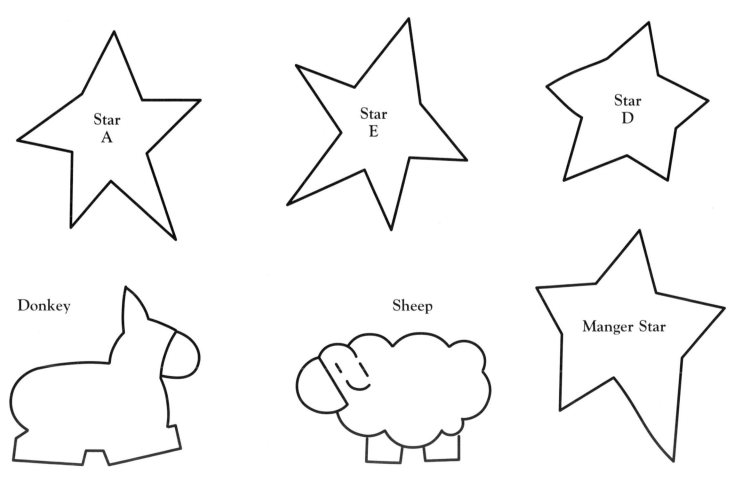

Star A

Star E

Star D

Donkey

Sheep

Manger Star

Mary's Headdress

Joseph's Headdress

Mary's/Joseph's Face

Figure

Halo

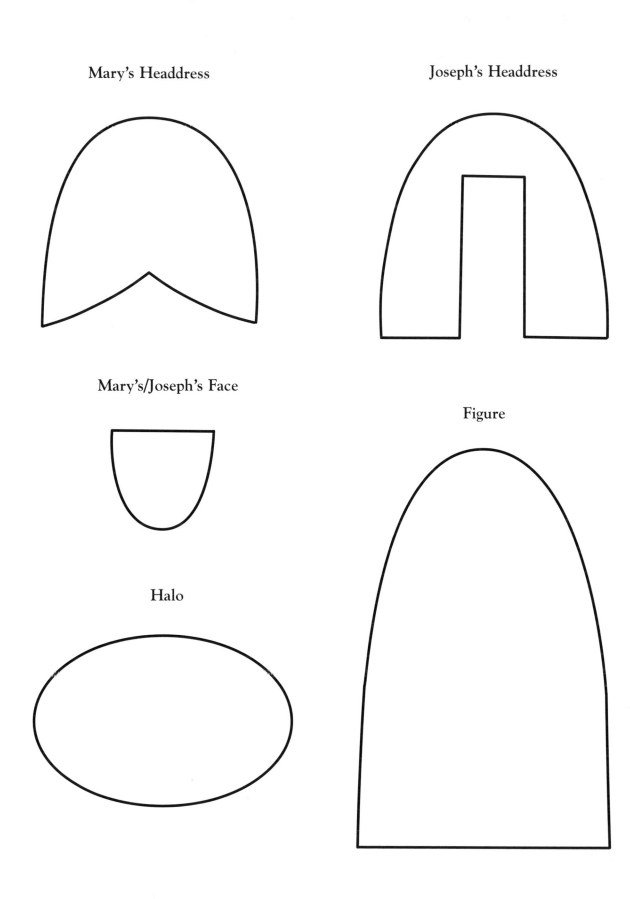

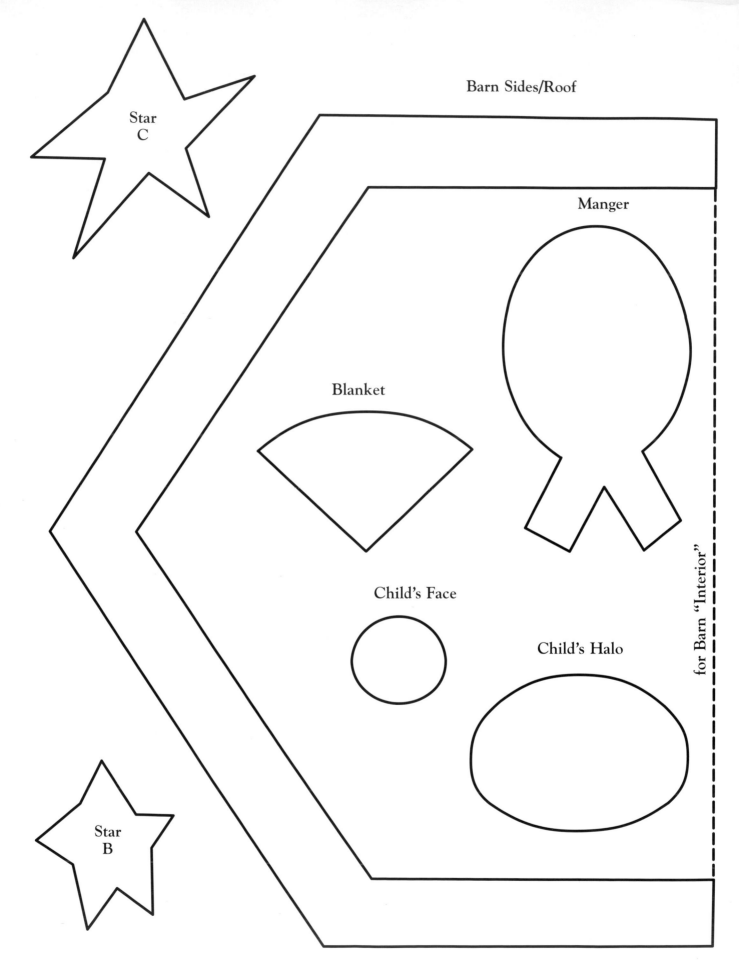

Star
C

Barn Sides/Roof

Manger

Blanket

Child's Face

Child's Halo

for Barn "Interior"

Star
B

112

santa collection
(pages 16-19)

Jolly Santa Doll (Continued)

Pin/stitch beard pieces together, leaving top open for turning; turn. Stuff; baste closed. Pin basted edge of beard in neck opening; stitch. *Hat* – Fold hatband in half lengthwise, right sides out, edges even; pin along fold. Pin band along bottom edge of right side of hat; stitch. Fold hat in half, edges even; pin. Stitch hat from point to band, leaving seam at band open. Pin/stitch hat to head.

Finishing: Turn Santa doll right side out through opening at back. Stuff doll till body is firm, using a dowel to push stuffing down into hands and boots. Close off top half of hat with pins to keep it *unstuffed*. (Tip of hat will be folded down after stuffing.) Stitch opening closed. Lightly stuff hatband; stitch closed.

Details: *Nose* – With wrong side of fabric facing you, turn fabric under ¼", taking small running stitches as you go. Pull up stitches to partially gather opening; stuff; gather tightly; tie thread ends in double knot. *Pom-pom* – Make same as nose.
Hat – Remove pins from hat; fold down point (see photo); pin/stitch pom-pom securely to hatband. *Face* – Brush blush on cheeks. Pin/stitch mustache pieces together, leaving opening (dash line on pattern) for turning; turn. Stuff; stitch closed. Sew to face just above beard. Sew on dome buttons for eyes, or for a very young child, embroider eyes at X's. Stitch on pom-pom nose securely (where shown on pattern). *Belt* – Fold belt lengthwise in half (bring edges to middle). Pin/stitch to jacket just above jacket skirt. Glue buckle pieces together (double thickness); glue or stitch to belt at front of jacket. *Sack* – Fold green velvet rectangle in half (10" x 11"), right sides facing. Sew sides using ¼" seam allowance. Fold down top edge 1"; stitch a ½" casing. Snip stitches in one side seam for casing opening. Thread shoelace through casing; knot ends of shoelace. Turn sack right side out. Fill with small gift-wrapped boxes.

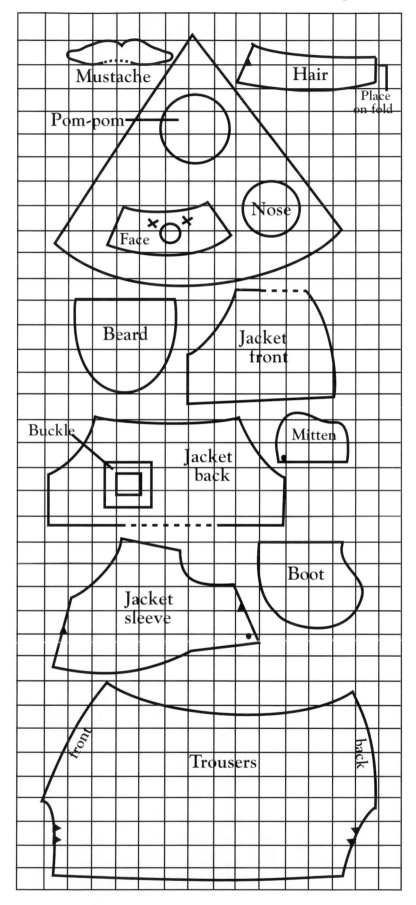

1 square=1"

Saint Nick Letter Box

You need: Shoe box; kraft paper; craft glue; medium-point permanent black marker; several yards jute twine; craft knife; 18" x 16" mat board; ½ yd red felt; felt scraps – white, pink, black, tan, green; white terrycloth scrap; 10" x 2" piece cut from red-and-white-checked dishtowel; two ¾" black buttons; 2" white pom-pom.

Preparing box: Discard box lid. Wrap box with kraft paper, folding edges to inside; glue edges inside box. Use marker to draw "postmark" on front of box (see photo). Glue twine to box front, wrapping and gluing ends to inside.

Making patterns: Enlarge Santa and mitten patterns so bottom edge of Santa (beard) is width of box; mitten is 2" longer than depth of box.

Cutting: *From mat board* – Trace patterns; cut one Santa and two mittens (following inner line) using craft knife. *From red felt* – Cut four mittens (following outer line on pattern), one nose, and one hat. *From white felt* – Cut two 2" x 1" strips for eyelashes; cut fringe on edges. *From pink felt* – Cut two cheeks. *From black felt* – Cut two eyes. *From tan felt* – Cut one face. *From green felt* – Cut two of each shape of mitten trim. *From terrycloth* – Cut one mustache; cut fringe on edges. *From dishtowel* – Cut one hatband.

Assembling: Glue felt mittens to each side of mat board mittens, raw edges even. Glue mitten trims to one side of each mitten. Glue remaining felt and fabric shapes to one side of Santa, curving eyelashes (see photo). Glue buttons over felt eyes. Glue pom-pom to tip of hat. Glue Santa to back of box. Glue mittens to sides of box, trimmed side out.

Tinted Santa Card Illustration

The publisher grants permission to the owner of this book to photocopy this illustration for personal use only.

Santa Centerpiece (Continued)

Trim top of cone to fit into opening of Santa head if needed. Glue head to top of cone.

Making each arm: Center and glue an 8" length of floral wire to one short edge of a 5" x 12" batting piece. Roll batting tightly around wire; glue. Glue one hand to one wire end. Glue remaining wire end into side of cone.

Making robe: *When sewing, match right sides and use a ¼" seam unless noted.* Cut a 20" x 32" fabric piece. Fold in half from top to bottom and again from left to right. Use compass and a straight edge to draw cutting lines as shown in *Diagram*. Cut out through all layers. Unfold fabric once. Sew sleeve and side seams; turn. Hand baste along neck and sleeve edges. Place robe on Santa. Gather robe at neck and sleeves; knot threads. Glue ribbon over each raw edge of sleeve. Fold bottom edge of robe loosely to bottom of cone; glue. Cut a cardboard circle slightly smaller than bottom of cone; glue to cone.

Making coat: Cut a 17½" x 26" fabric piece. Fold, cut, and stitch in same manner as robe. Cut center opening through one layer from center bottom to neck opening. Press all raw edges except neck edge under ¼"; glue. Hand baste along neck edge.

Making hat: Fold hat fabric in half. Use full-size hat pattern to cut hat from fabric. Sew straight edges together to form a cone; turn. Press raw edge of hat under ¼"; glue. Sew jingle bell to hat.

Adding fur trim: Using craft knife and cutting through back of fur only, cut the following 1½"W fur strips: 22½", 7", two 12", two 10". Cut a 1" x 10" strip. Fold long edges of strips under ¼"; glue. Glue 1" x 10" strip to bottom edge of hat. Glue strips to coat as follows: 22½" strip to bottom edge, 12" strips along center front edges, 10" strips along sleeve edges. Place coat on Santa. Gather coat at neck; knot thread. Glue 7" strip over neck edge. Use liner brush and fabric dye to lightly paint small sections of fur on coat to look like ermine.

Adding hair and beard: For hair and beard, cut 3"-6" lengths of doll hair. Fold each length in half; glue fold to face. For mustache, cut a 3" length; wrap center with white sewing thread. Glue to face. Lightly brush and trim hair as desired.

Making bag: Cut a 6½" x 15" muslin piece. *Stitching* – Matching short edges, fold muslin in half (fold is bottom of sack). Sew side edges. Press top edge under ¾"; stitch ½" from fold for casing; turn. Cut a small slit in casing. Thread twine through casing, gathering top of bag slightly; knot close to bag. *Stiffening* – Saturate bag with fabric stiffener. Stuff bag lightly with crumpled pieces of foil, shaping bag as desired. Let dry. Remove foil. *Painting* – Spray bag with paint. Paint highlights on prominent folds of bag using light red paint.

Finishing: Wrap small boxes with wrapping paper and curling ribbon. Fill bag with excelsior. Glue hat on head and pipe to mouth. Arrange arms, gluing tree to one hand and one gift package to other. Arrange Santa, bag, extra packages, and holly sprigs on a layer of stuffing sprinkled with artificial snow.

Cutting Diagram

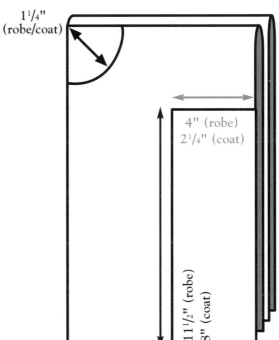

1¼"
(robe/coat)

4" (robe)
2¼" (coat)

11½" (robe)
8" (coat)

Place on fold of fabric

Hat

Nostalgic Santa Pillow

Pillow size: 16" x 13¾"

You need: 22" x 20" piece of 10 mesh needlepoint canvas; ½ yd fabric for pillow back; Persian yarn; 3" x 1⅔ yds bias fabric strip; 1⅔ yds of ⅜" cord; #22 tapestry needle; stuffing.

Stitching design: Work one tent stitch to correspond to each square in chart. Work design on canvas using two strands of yarn. Complete background of design as noted in key. Clean and block completed design.

Making pillow: *Front –* Trim canvas to ½" from stitched design. Cut pillow back same size as pillow front. *Welting –* Press one end of bias strip ½" to wrong side. Center cord on wrong side of bias strip. Matching long edges, fold strip over cord. Using zipper foot, baste close to cord; trim seam allowance to ⅝". Pin welting to right side of pillow front, clipping seam allowance at corners. Overlap ends of welting 1" and trim excess. Remove basting from 1" of finished end of welting and trim ends of cord to fit. Overlap pressed end of fabric over unfinished end of welting; baste ends in place. *Finishing –* Place pillow front and back right sides together. Leaving an opening for turning, use zipper foot to sew front and back together. Turn, stuff, and sew closed.

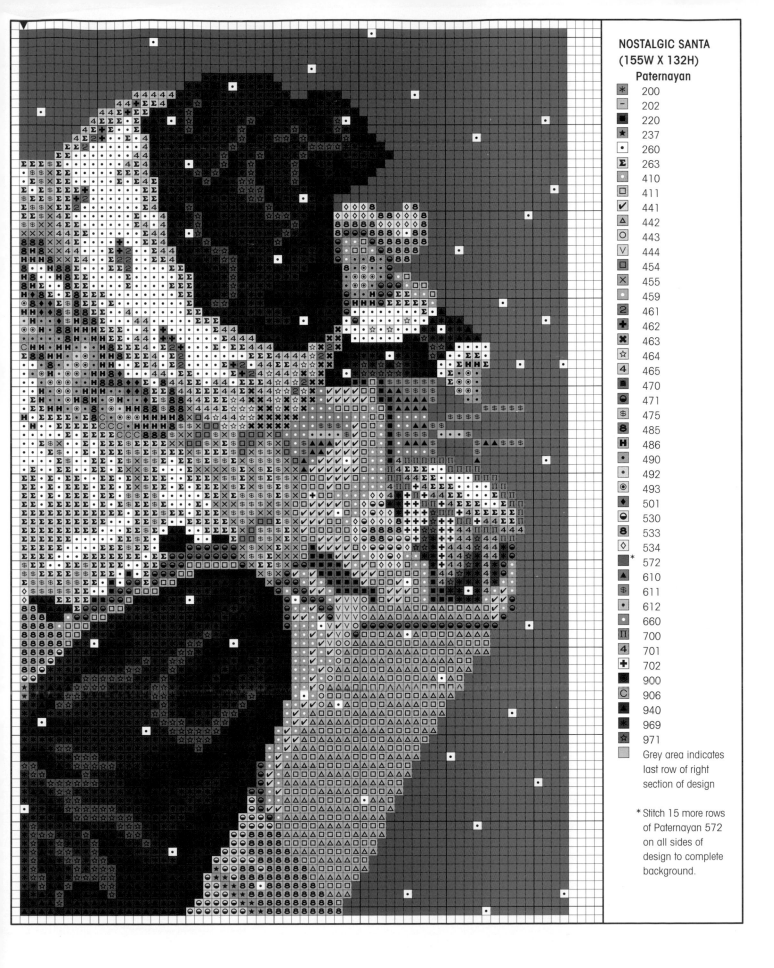

NOSTALGIC SANTA
(155W X 132H)
Paternayan

Symbol	Color
✳	200
−	202
■	220
★	237
•	260
Σ	263
⊙	410
□	411
✔	441
△	442
O	443
V	444
▱	454
✕	455
⊡	459
2	461
✚	462
✖	463
☆	464
4	465
▪	470
⊖	471
$	475
8	485
H	486
•	490
•	492
◉	493
◆	501
⊖	530
8	533
◇	534
■ *	572
▲	610
$	611
•	612
•	660
Π	700
4	701
✚	702
■	900
C	906
■	940
✳	969
☆	971

Grey area indicates last row of right section of design

* Stitch 15 more rows of Paternayan 572 on all sides of design to complete background.

117

country charm (pages 18-23)
Papier-mâché Santa

You need: 9"h plastic foam cone; instant papier-mâché; acrylic paint – white, ivory, light yellow, dark yellow, peach, dark red, brown, dark brown, green, blue; white gesso; paintbrushes; toothpicks; spray acrylic sealer; craft glue.

Preparing: Mix papier-mâché in a bowl. Spread a thin layer of glue over sides and top of cone.

Sculpting: *See Diagram and apply papier-mâché as follows when sculpting.* Spread a smooth 1/8" layer of papier-mâché over glue. *Hat top* – Build up top of cone 1/2". *Face* – Use toothpick to outline a 1 1/2" circle 2 1/4" from top of Santa. *Hat fur trim* – Apply a 5 1/4"L, 3/8" thick roll to cone. *Beard* – Form a 1/4" thick beard shape; apply. *Hair* – Apply a 1/4" thick layer along sides of face and to back of head. *Nose and mustache* – Form nose and mustache from small pieces; apply. *Arms* – Apply a 2"L, 3/4" thick roll to each side of Santa. *Sleeve trims* – Apply a 1"L, 3/8" thick roll 1/2" from bottom of each arm. *Mittens* – Use toothpick to separate thumb from hand at bottom of each arm. *Bottom of coat* – Apply a 10 3/4"L, 3/8" thick roll to cone along bottom edge. *Bag* – Form a 1/4" thick bag shape; apply to coat, connecting top of bag to mitten.

Texturing: Use toothpick to add texture to mustache, beard, hair, and fur trims.

Drying: Place in front of a fan to dry. (Drying may take two days or longer.)

Preparing for painting: Apply one coat of gesso to Santa. To give hat and coat an antique look, apply an undercoat of light yellow paint to hat and coat.

Basecoating: Apply dark red basecoat on top of yellow undercoat, allowing edges of yellow to show through. Basecoat mustache, beard, hair, and fur trims ivory; face peach; mittens green; and bag dark yellow.

Painting details: Paint mouth dark red, eyes blue, eyebrows white, and stars on bag dark brown.

Shading: Thin brown paint slightly with water. Use mixture to outline fur trims, bottom of beard, bag, and mittens. Use undiluted dark brown paint to outline arms.

Highlighting: Highlight eyes, mustache, beard, hair, and fur trims with white paint.

Antiquing: Spray Santa with two coats of acrylic sealer. Thin brown paint with water. Working on one area at a time, apply mixture to mustache, beard, hair, fur trims, and bag; use a soft cloth to wipe away excess. Spray Santa with two more coats of acrylic sealer.

3-D Ginger Men Ornaments

You need (to make 10-ornament garland): Glue stick; sheets of decorative paper – brown embossed, 2 tan prints; lightweight cardboard; gingerbread-man cookie cutter; craft knife; glue gun; several yards of striped cotton cord.

Preparing cardboard: Using glue stick, glue embossed paper to one side of cardboard. Cut cardboard in half; glue one piece of printed paper to other side of each cardboard piece.

Making ornaments: Trace cookie cutter 20 times onto cardboard; cut out ginger men. Make vertical slits in 10 ginger men from top of head to center of body. Make vertical slits in remaining ginger men from lower edge to center of body.

Finishing: Fit two gingermen together at slits, alternating paper prints and textures, to make ornament. Make remaining ornaments in same way. Using glue gun, attach ornaments, evenly spaced, to cord.

Santa Diagram

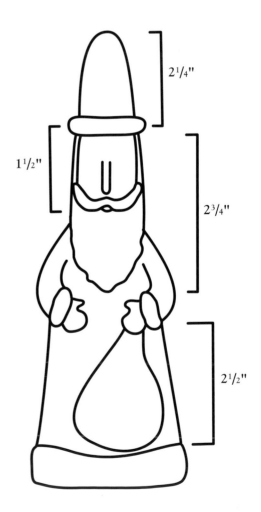

Ginger Skater

You need: Transfer paper; 14" of 1" x 12" pine; C-clamps; hand-held electric jigsaw; sandpaper; sheet of acetate; craft knife; fine paintbrush; acrylic paints – black, red; sponge.

Cutting: Enlarge pattern to 14" tall. Transfer skater outline onto wood. Clamp wood onto work surface; cut with jigsaw. Sand all edges. Transfer heart onto acetate; using craft knife, cut out center of heart to make stencil.

Painting: Using brush, paint face, stripes, and skates; let dry. Place stencil on skater. Pounce sponge in red paint, then inside stencil. Let dry.

Note: If desired, use enlarged pattern to make giant Ginger Skater cookies. Use Gingerbread Dough (page 85), rolled to about ¹/₄" thick; bake as directed. Use Royal Icing (page 85) to ice as on photo.

Ginger Skater
Enlarge to 14" tall

snow pals (pages 24-25)

Mitten Ornaments

You need (for each): 6" x 8" piece of Oatmeal Floba (14 ct); embroidery floss (see key); needle; 6" x 8" piece of backing fabric; 6" of ¼"W ribbon.

Stitching: Work design on Floba using four strands of floss for cross stitches and two strands for backstitches and French knots.

Cutting: Place stitched design and backing fabric right sides together. Draw around full-size pattern on wrong side of stitched design.

Sewing: Leaving top edge open, sew directly on drawn line, backstitching at beginning and end of seam. Trim top edge along drawn line and trim seam allowance to ¼". Clip curves and turn.

Finishing: Press top edge of mitten ½" to wrong side. Use six strands of floss work to blanket stitches along top edge of mitten. For hanger, fold ribbon in half and tack ends to inside of mitten at seam.

Mitten

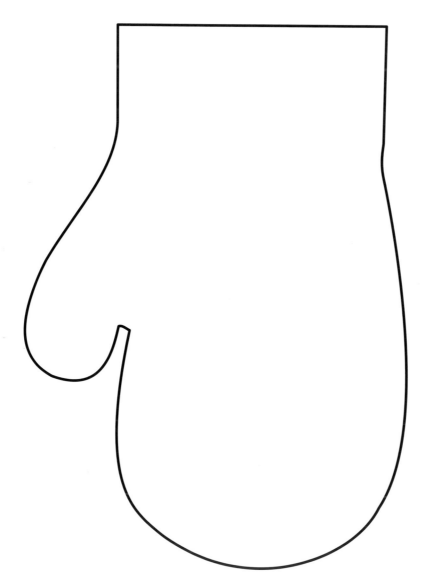

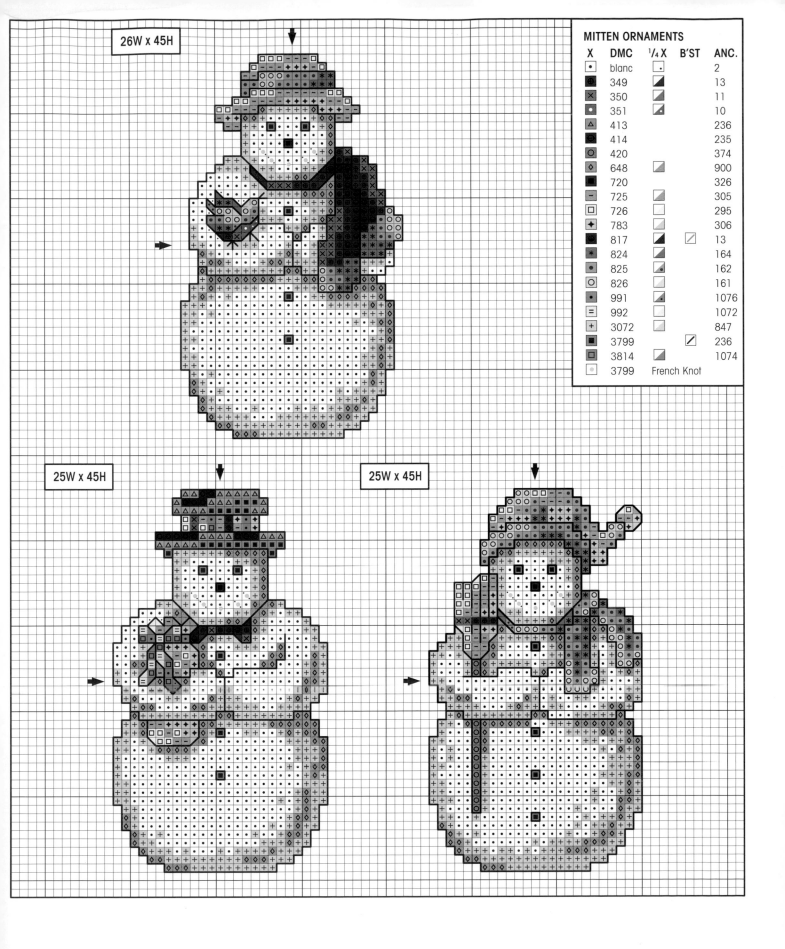

26W x 45H

25W x 45H

25W x 45H

MITTEN ORNAMENTS

X	DMC	¼ X	B'ST	ANC.
•	blanc	•		2
⊕	349	◤		13
✕	350	◤		11
⊡	351	◢		10
△	413			236
▣	414			235
◯	420			374
◇	648	◤		900
▪	720			326
−	725	◤		305
□	726	◻		295
✦	783	◤		306
▨	817	◤	◿	13
✳	824	◤		164
◉	825	◢		162
◎	826	◤		161
●	991	◤		1076
=	992	◻		1072
+	3072	◻		847
▦	3799		◿	236
▤	3814	◤		1074
◌	3799		French Knot	

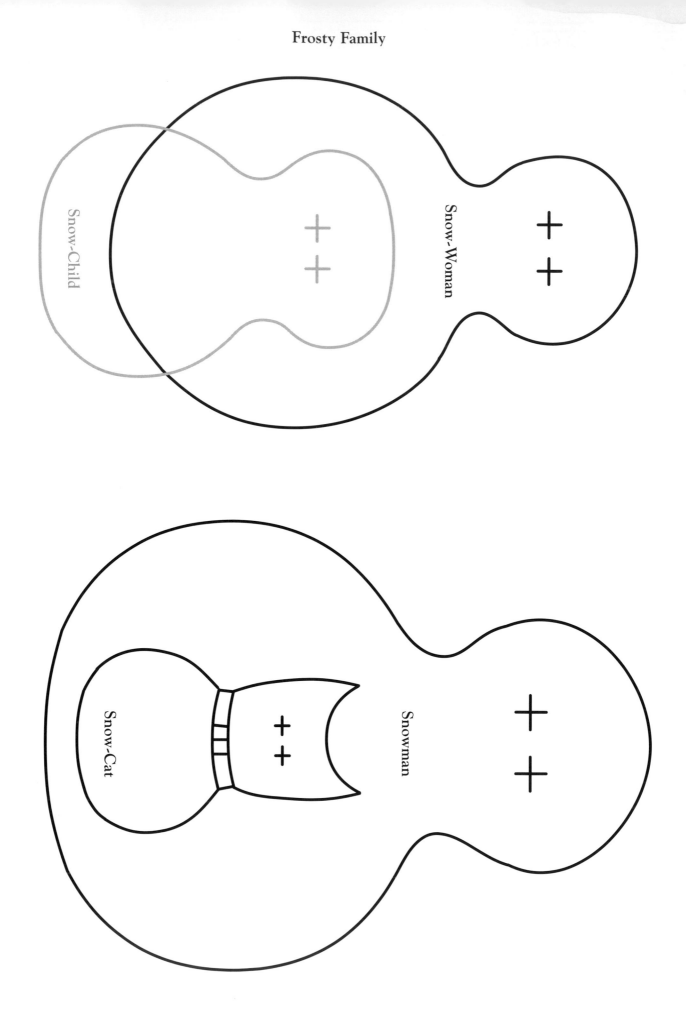

Snow-Child

Snow-Woman

Snow-Cat

Snowman

a season for stitching
(pages 26-29)

Santa Portrait

You need: 13" x 14" Ivory Lugana (25 ct); embroidery floss (see key); needle.
Stitching: Stitch design over two fabric threads using three strands of floss for cross stitches and one strand for half cross stitches, backstitches, and French knots.
Finishing: Frame design in a custom frame.

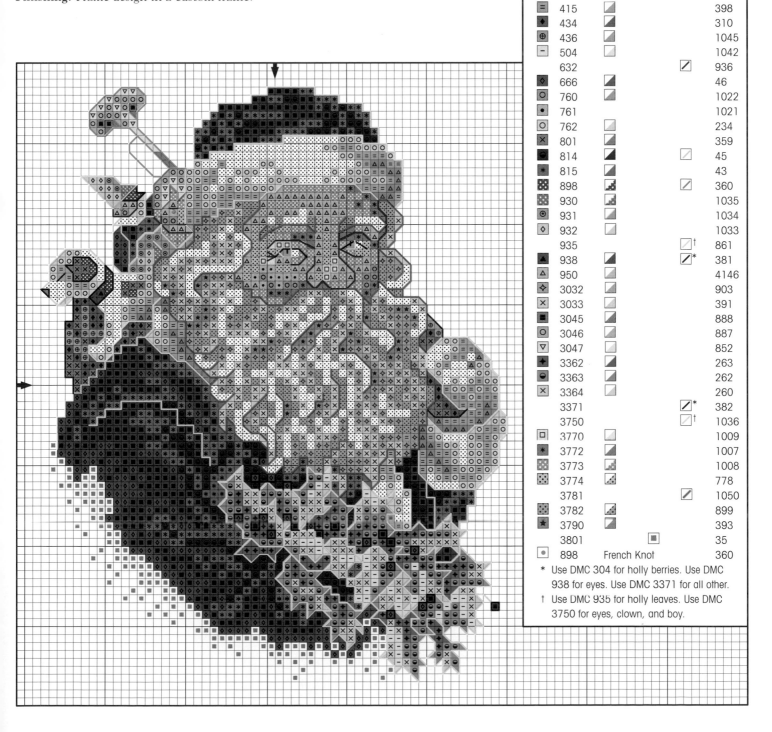

X	DMC	¼X	½X	B'ST	ANC.
⋰	blanc	⋰			2
■	304	◢		╱*	1006
▲	318	◢			399
	414			╱	235
=	415	◢			398
◆	434	◢			310
⊕	436	◢			1045
-	504	◢			1042
	632			╱	936
◈	666	◢			46
○	760	◢			1022
•	761				1021
○	762	◢			234
✕	801	◢			359
◨	814	◢		╱	45
✳	815	◢			43
▦	898	◢		╱	360
▩	930	◢			1035
◉	931	◢			1034
◇	932	◢			1033
	935			╱†	861
▲	938	◢		╱*	381
△	950	◢			4146
◆	3032	◢			903
✕	3033	◢			391
▪	3045	◢			888
○	3046	◢			887
▽	3047	◢			852
◆	3362	◢			263
◖	3363	◢			262
✕	3364	◢			260
	3371			╱*	382
	3750			╱†	1036
☐	3770	◢			1009
✳	3772	◢			1007
▨	3773	◢			1008
⋰	3774	◢			778
	3781			╱	1050
▨	3782	◢			899
★	3790	◢			393
	3801		▪		35
⊙	898	French Knot			360

* Use DMC 304 for holly berries. Use DMC 938 for eyes. Use DMC 3371 for all other.
† Use DMC 935 for holly leaves. Use DMC 3750 for eyes, clown, and boy.

Mini Stockings

You need (for each): Two 8" x 10" pieces of Raw Belfast Linen (32 ct); ⅓ yd fabric for lining and cording; embroidery floss (see key); needle; ½ yd of ⅛" dia. cord.

Stitching: Stitch design on one linen piece over two fabric threads using two strands of floss for cross stitches, one strand for half cross stitches, one strand for backstitches, and one for French knots.

Cutting pieces: *Stocking* – Place stitched piece and second linen piece right sides together. Center full-size pattern over stitched design; cut out stocking pieces through both layers. *Hanger* – Cut one 1" x 3½" strip from linen scraps. *Lining* – Fold fabric in half and use pattern to cut two lining pieces. *Cording* – Cut one 2" x 18" bias fabric strip.

Adding cording: Center cord on wrong side of fabric strip; fold strip over cord. Baste along strip close to cord; trim seam allowance to ¼". Baste cording to right side of stitched piece along side and bottom edges.

Sewing stocking and lining: With right sides facing and using a ¼" seam allowance, sew stitched piece and linen stocking piece together; turn. Press top edge ½" to wrong side. Repeat for lining pieces; do not turn lining right side out.

Adding hanger: Press long edges of fabric strip ¼" to center. Press strip in half lengthwise and sew close to folded edges. Matching short edges, fold hanger in half and whipstitch to inside of stocking.

Finishing: Place lining inside stocking. Whipstitch lining to stocking along pressed edge.

Stocking

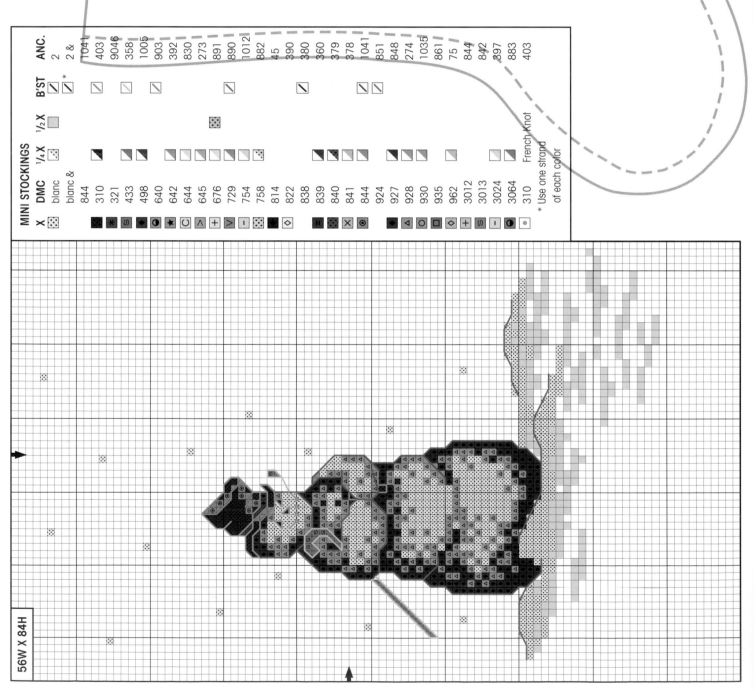

56W x 84H

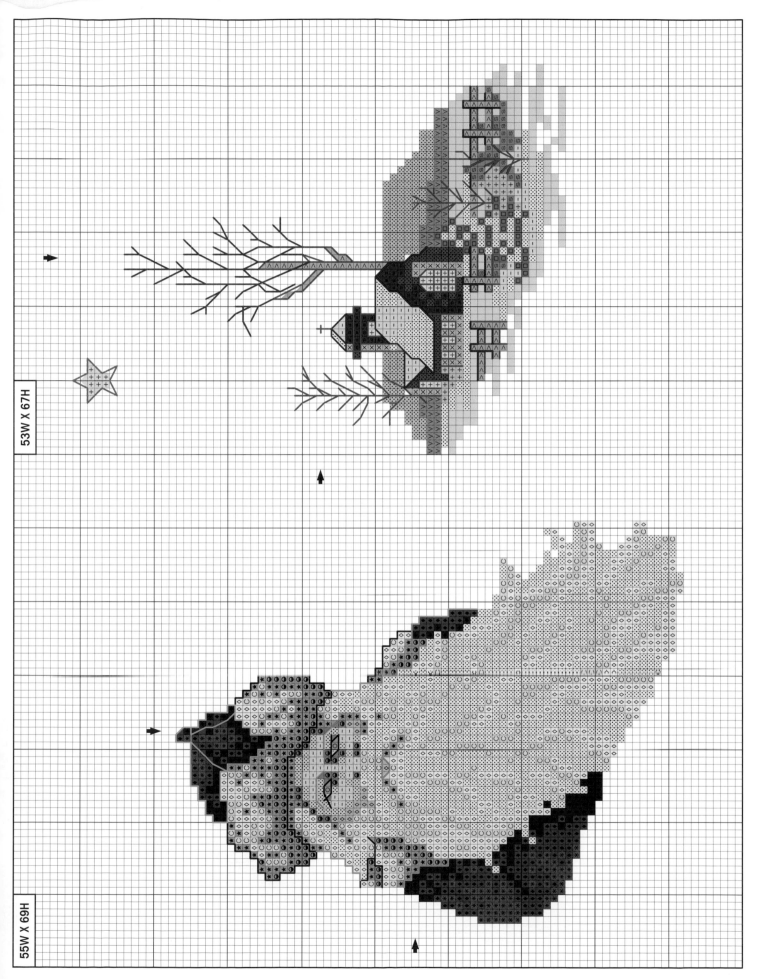

53W X 67H

55W X 69H

"Merry Christmas to All" Pillow

You need: 13" x 10" Parchment Hearthstone (14 ct); embroidery floss (see key); needle; fabrics – ½ yd for backing and ruffle, ½ yd for cording; ⅞ yd of ¼" dia. cord; stuffing.

Stitching: Stitch design using three strands of floss for cross stitches and two strands for backstitches. Trim finished design to 9" x 6¾".

Finishing: *Cording* – Cut a 2" x 29" bias strip from cording fabric, piecing as needed. Center cord on wrong side of bias strip; fold strip over cord. Baste along strip close to cord; trim seam allowance to ½". Baste cording to right side of stitched piece. *Ruffle* – Cut a 5½" x 56" strip from ruffle fabric, piecing as needed. Matching right sides, sew short ends together. Press in half, wrong sides facing. Baste ½" and ¼" from raw edges; gather fabric to fit stitched piece. Baste ruffle to right side of stitched piece. *Backing* – Cut a 9" x 6¾" fabric piece. Match right sides of stitched piece and backing fabric. Sew using a ½" seam allowance and leaving an opening for turning; turn. Stuff pillow and stitch opening closed.

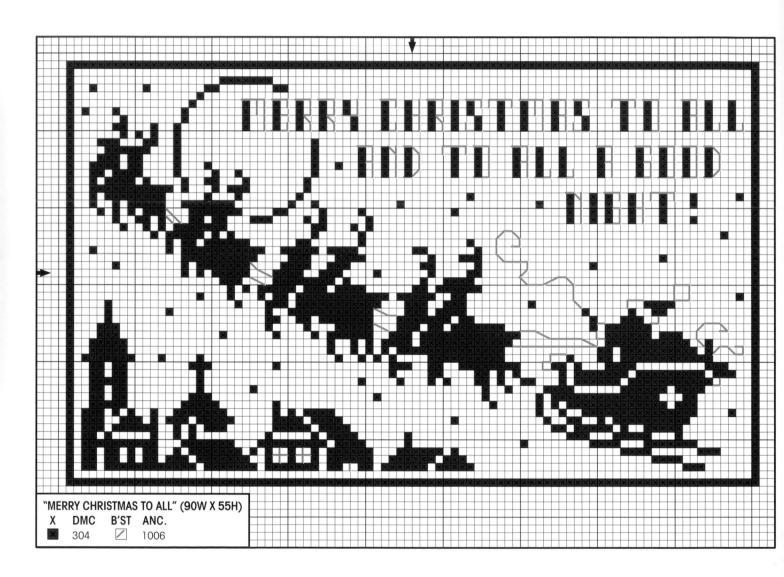

"MERRY CHRISTMAS TO ALL" (90W X 55H)

X	DMC	B'ST	ANC.
■	304	╱	1006

Snowflake Sweatshirt

You need: Sweatshirt; embroidery floss (see key); needle; 23" x 10" piece of 8.5 mesh waste canvas; 23" x 10" piece of lightweight non-fusible interfacing; embroidery hoop.

Preparing sweatshirt: Baste waste canvas to sweatshirt front; baste interfacing to inside of sweatshirt under canvas. Place sweatshirt in hoop.

Stitching design: With large snowflake centered horizontally, stitch design, repeating as needed. Use six strands of floss for cross stitches.

Finishing: Trim canvas to ¾" from design. Dampen canvas slightly to remove sizing. Use tweezers to pull out canvas threads. Trim interfacing close to design.

Poinsettia Ornament

You need: 7" x 9" Antique White Aida (18 ct); embroidery floss (see key); needle; purchased frame with 2¼" x 2½" opening.

Stitching: Stitch design using two strands of floss for cross stitches and one strand for backstitches and French knots.

Finishing: Insert design in frame.

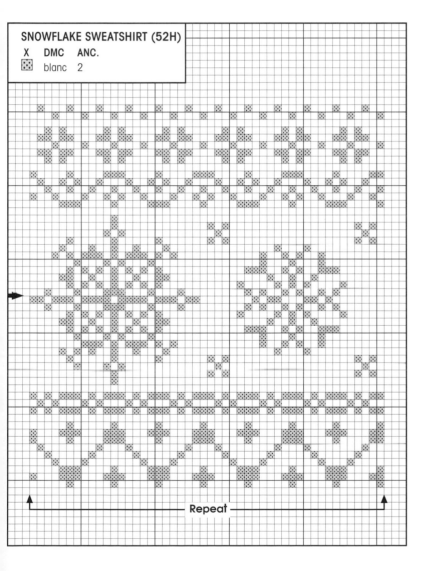

SNOWFLAKE SWEATSHIRT (52H)

X	DMC	ANC.
⊠	blanc	2

Repeat

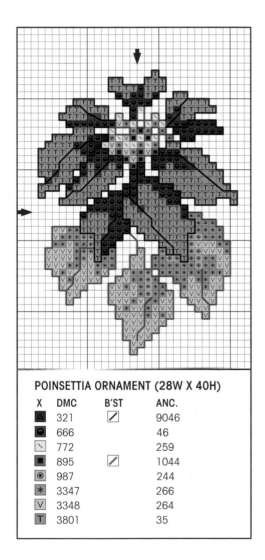

POINSETTIA ORNAMENT (28W X 40H)

X	DMC	B'ST	ANC.
▲	321	╱	9046
◐	666		46
◸	772		259
▪	895	╱	1044
⊙	987		244
✳	3347		266
∨	3348		264
T	3801		35

127

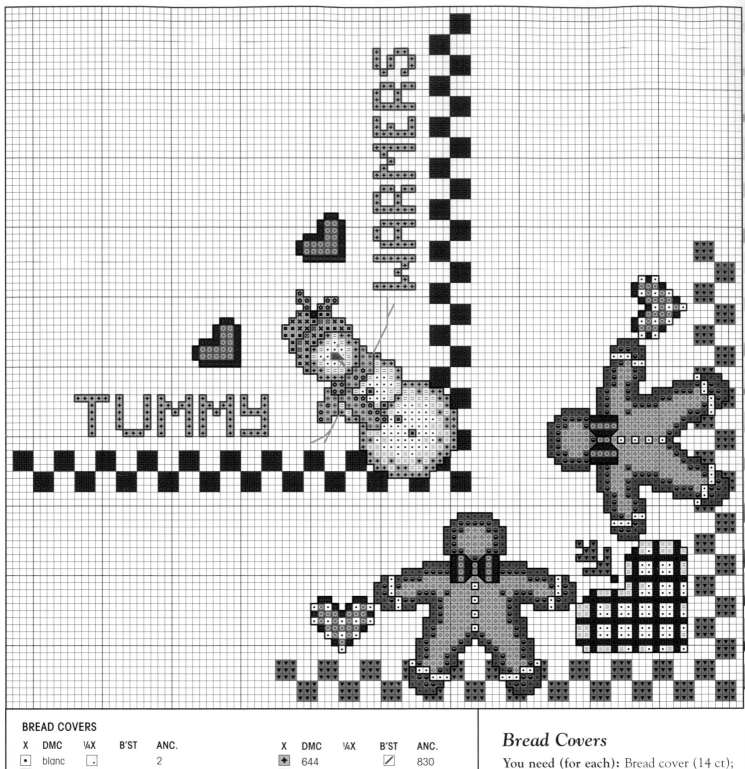

BREAD COVERS

X	DMC	¼X	B'ST	ANC.		X	DMC	¼X	B'ST	ANC.
·	blanc	·		2		✦	644		◢	830
◼	304	◢		1006		⊠	645			273
◼	310		◢	403			720		◢	326
▼	319			218		△	722	◢		323
⬠	320			215		◼	814			45
○	321			9046		=	822			390
◉	367			217		✖	844			1041
✳	434		◢ *	310		●	310		French Knot	
◕	435	◢		1046		*Use 3 strands of floss.				
◈	436	◢		1045						

Bread Covers

You need (for each): Bread cover (14 ct); embroidery floss (see key); needle.

Stitching: Stitch design on one corner of bread cover four squares from beginning of fringe on each side. Use three strands of floss for cross stitches and one strand for backstitches and French knots unless noted. Continue stitching borders along edges of bread cover.

Log Cabin Sweatshirt

You need: Sweatshirt; embroidery floss (see key); needle; 13" x 12" piece of 8.5 mesh waste canvas; 13" x 12" piece of lightweight non-fusible interfacing; embroidery hoop.

Preparing sweatshirt: Baste waste canvas to sweatshirt front; baste interfacing to inside of sweatshirt under canvas. Place sweatshirt in hoop.

Stitching design: Stitch design using six strands of floss for cross stitches, six strands for backstitches, and two strands for French knots.

Finishing: Trim canvas to ¾" from design. Dampen canvas slightly to remove sizing. Use tweezers to pull out canvas threads. Trim interfacing close to design.

LOG CABIN SWEATSHIRT
(73W x 67H)

X	DMC	B'ST	ANC.
⊙	ecru	╱	387
✳	321		9046
C	433		358
+	436		1045
□	562		210
S	648		900
-	725		305
•	ecru French Knot		387
•	310 French Knot		403

129

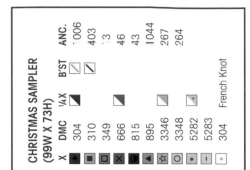

CHRISTMAS SAMPLER (99W X 73H)										
X	DMC	ANC.	B'ST	¼X						French Knot
	304	006								
	310	403								
	349	3								
	666	46								
	815	43								
	895	1044								
	3346	267								
	3348	264								
	5282									
	5283									
	304									

Christmas Sampler

You need: 10" x 12" Ivory Monaco (28 ct); embroidery floss (see key); needle; 8" x 10" wooden frame; saber saw; primer; red gloss spray enamel; ribbon.

Stitching: Work design over two fabric threads using two strands of floss for cross stitches and one strand for backstitches.

Framing: Draw a scalloped line around outer edge of frame; cut along line with saber saw. Prime, then paint frame. Insert design in painted frame. Add ribbon bows to frame.

Tea-dyed Angel (Continued)

Heart: With right sides facing, sandwich gathered lace between linen and velvet heart pieces. Stitch front to back. Clip curves and trim. Make small slit in linen (back of heart) as indicated by arrow on pattern and turn. Stuff heart and stitch closed. Stitch buttons to front of heart and stitch heart to extended hands.

Finishing: Attach $1^1/_2$"W lace to bottom of dress at hem line using fabric glue; attach $^3/_4$"W lace to neckline. Crisscross ribbon up each leg and secure with stitch through bow at back. Paint eyes and mouth; color cheeks with blush. Hot glue wreath on head for halo.

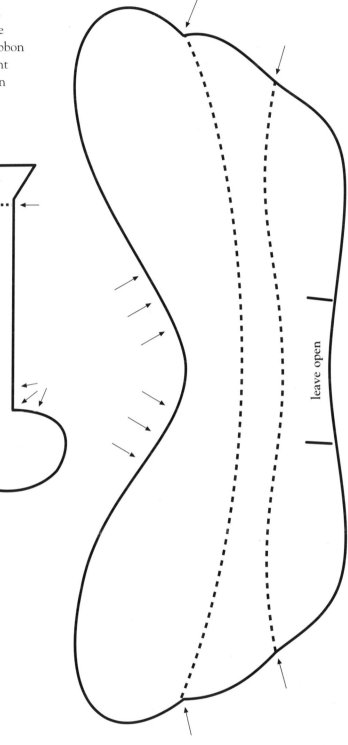

Arm

Leg

Heart

Wings

leave open

Doll

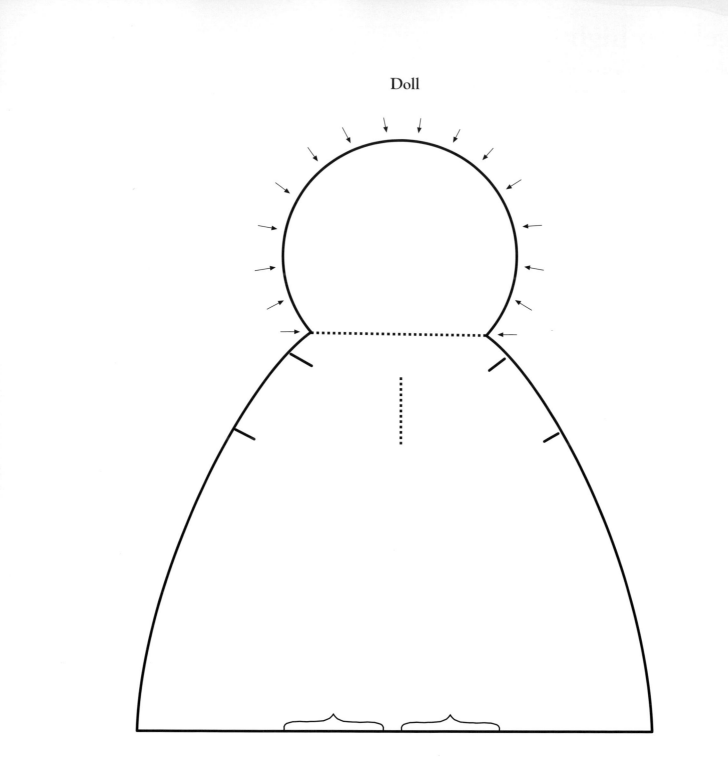

Dress

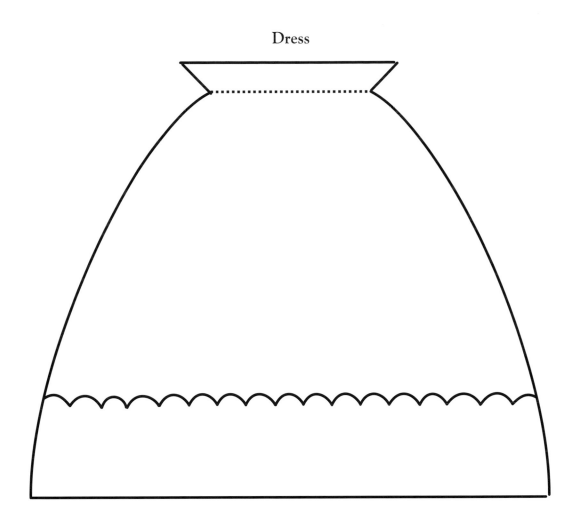

Crocheted Angel

You need: Bedspread weight cotton thread – approx. 36 yds; steel crochet hook – size 5 (1.90 mm); 12" of 1/8"W ribbon; 3¼" round, slotted clothespin; craft glue.

Gauge: 16 dc and 8 rows = 2".

BODICE

Leaving an 18" length at beginning for Neck Edging, ch 14 **loosely**; being careful not to twist ch, join with slip st to form a ring.

Rnd 1(Right side): Ch 3 **(counts as first dc, now and throughout)**, dc in same st, 2 dc in next ch, ★ ch 1 **(dc, ch 1)** 3 times in next ch, (dc, ch 1) twice in next ch, (dc, ch 1) 3 times in next ch ★, 2 dc in each of next 4 chs, repeat from ★ to ★ once, 2 dc in each of last 2 chs; join with slip st to first dc: 32 dc.

Note: Loop a short piece of thread around any stitch to mark last round as **right** side.

Rnd 2: Ch 3, dc in next 3 dc, ch 1, skip next 9 ch-1 sps (Armhole), dc in next 8 dc, ch 1, skip next 9 ch-1 sps

(Armhole), dc in last 4 dc; join with slip st to first dc: 16 dc.

SKIRT

Rnd 1: Ch 6, working in each dc and in each ch around, dc in next st, ★ (ch 3, dc) twice in next st, (ch 3, dc in next st) 3 times, (ch 3, dc) twice in next st ★, (ch 3, dc in next st) 4 times, repeat from ★ to ★ once, (ch 3, dc in next st) twice, ch 1, dc in third ch of beginning ch-6 to form last sp: 22 sps.

Rnd 2: Sc in same sp, ch 4, (sc, ch 3, 2 dc) in next ch-3 sp, ★ sc in next ch-3 sp, ch 4, (sc, ch 3, 2 dc) in next ch-3 sp; repeat from ★ around; join with slip st to first sc.

Rnds 3-8: Slip st in first 2 chs, sc in same ch-4 sp, ch 4, (sc, ch 3, 2 dc) in next ch-3 sp; ★ sc in next ch-4 sp, ch 4, (sc, ch 3, 2 dc) in next ch-3 sp; repeat from ★ around; join with slip st to first sc.

Edging: Ch 3, 2 dc in same sp, (sc, ch 3, 2 dc) in next ch-sp and in each ch-sp around; join with slip st to first ch, fasten off.

WING (make 2)

Rnd 1: With **right** side facing and working in free loop of ch-1 **and** in skipped ch-1 sps of Armhole, join with sc in ch-1 at underarm; ch 3, sc around post of next dc, ch 3, (sc in next ch-1 sp, ch 3) 9 times, sc around post of next dc, ch 1, dc in first sc to form last sp: 12 sps.

Rnds 2 and 3: Sc in same sp, (ch 3, sc in next ch-3 sp) around, ch 1, dc in first sc to form last sp.

To work Cluster, ch 3, YO, insert hook in third ch from hook, YO and pull up a loop, YO and draw through 2 loops on hook, YO, insert hook in **same** ch, YO and pull up a loop, YO and draw through 2 loops on hook, YO and draw through all 3 loops on hook.

Rnd 4: Sc in same sp, work Cluster, (sc in next ch-3 sp, work Cluster) around; join with slip st to first sc, fasten off.

FINISHING

Neck edging: With **right** side facing and working in free loops of beginning ch, insert hook in same ch as joining, using beginning length, YO and pull up a loop; (ch 1, slip st in next ch) around; fasten off.

Assembling: Weave ribbon through sts on Rnd 2 of Bodice. Place Dress over clothespin.

HALO

Rnd 1 (Right side): Ch 2, 8 sc in second ch from hook; join with slip st to first sc.

Rnd 2: Ch 1, sc in same st, (ch 3, sc in next sc) around, ch 1, dc in first sc to form last sp: 8 sps.

Rnd 3: Sc in same sp, ch 4, (sc in next ch-3 sp, ch 4) around; join with slip st to first sc, fasten off. Glue Halo to clothespin.

Muslin Angel

You need: Fabrics – muslin, scrap of red cotton fabric; stuffing; Spanish moss; fabric glue.

Tearing muslin: Tear muslin into one 6" x 10" piece for head/body and one 3" x 4" piece for wings.

Making angel: *Head/body* – Fold one long edge of 4½" x 7" muslin piece 1½" to back. Place a ¾" ball of stuffing between fabric layers at center of fold. Tie doubled thread tightly under stuffing **(Fig. 1)**. *Arms* – Knot each top fabric corner close to head. *Heart* – Use full-size pattern to cut heart from red fabric. Glue to angel.

Adding halo: Form a ring from a length of Spanish moss; glue to angel.

Adding wings: Form a bow shape by pinching together centers of long edges of remaining muslin piece; wrap with thread to secure. Overlap back edges of angel's skirt; secure with a dab of glue. Glue wings to angel.

Fig. 1

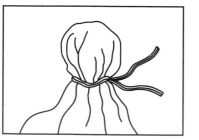

Heart

Cookie Angels

You need: Christmas-Tree Cookie dough (page 86); Royal Icing (page 85); lightweight cardboard; drinking straw; coarse sugar; silver dragées; paste food coloring; pastry bags; small writing tips.

Making cookies: Enlarge patterns as desired; trace onto cardboard and cut out. Roll out dough to ⅛" thickness. Place patterns on dough. Use tip of sharp knife to cut equal number of each shape from dough. Make a hole in top of each lady cookie using drinking straw. Bake in a preheated 375° oven for 6 minutes or until lightly browned on edges; cool.

Decorating: Spoon ¼ cup Royal Icing into each of three small bowls; cover with damp paper towel. Adding one teaspoon water at a time to remaining Royal Icing, thin icing to a spreading consistency (about one tablespoon water). Frost heart with untinted icing. Place lady cookie on top, without covering hanging hole. Sprinkle coarse sugar on wings; let air-dry. Frost angels; decorate with dragées. Let icing dry. Tint reserved icing yellow, blue, and red. Spoon icing into pastry bags fitted with small writing tips. Pipe tinted icing on head for hair, eyes, and mouth.

Note: Dragées are not recognized by the Food and Drug Administration as edible. Use for decoration only; remove dragées before eating cookies.

Enlarge patterns as desired

Lady

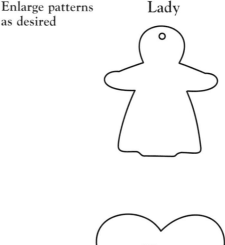

Heart

Pinecone Angel

You need: Pinecone (we used a 1½"W x 4"H cone); 2 silk leaves; hazelnut; 8" of ⅛"W gold silk ribbon; glue gun; gold spray paint.

To do: With glue gun, glue hazelnut to stem end of pinecone as head; glue leaves just below nut as wings; glue a ribbon hanger loop to back of cone. Spray-paint entire piece gold.

tree time (pages 34-35)

Felt Ornaments
Enlarge to 6" high

elegance from top to bottom (pages 36-37)

Star Tree Topper

You need: 12" of ½" x 12" pine; 4" wooden medallion; acrylic paint – ivory, gold metallic; sponge brush; sandpaper; floral wire; glue gun; saber saw.

Making star: Enlarge pattern. Trace the pattern on pine piece; cut out with saber saw. Glue wooden medallion to center of the star.

Painting: Paint star and medallion ivory. Then, when dry, paint gold. When gold is dry, sand gently so that some of the ivory paint shows through.

Finishing: Glue a piece of wire about 4" long to back of star to slip over treetop.

"Crazy-Quilt" Tree Skirt

You need: 44" square of muslin; fabric scraps; ½"W bias tape to coordinate with scraps; 3¾ yds each of 1"L gold fringe and ¼"W velvet ribbon; paper-backed fusible web; gold dimensional fabric-paint writer; fabric glue; removable fabric marking pen.

Covering muslin square: Fuse web to wrong sides of fabric scraps. Arrange scraps on muslin, trimming to fit; fuse in place.

Cutting tree skirt: Matching right sides, fold muslin square in half from top to bottom and again from left to right. *Outer cutting line* – Tie one end of string to fabric marking pen. Insert thumbtack through string 20½" from pen. Insert thumbtack in fabric as shown in *Fig. 1* and mark one-quarter of a circle. *Inner cutting line* – Repeat outer cutting line procedure, inserting thumbtack through string 1" from pen. Cut out tree skirt. *Skirt opening* – Cut through one layer of fabric along one fold line from outer to inner edge.

Painting: Use fabric-paint writer to add decorative "stitches" along raw edges of fabric scraps (see photo).

Finishing: Glue bias tape to opening edges and inner edge of skirt. Glue fringe to outer edge of skirt on right side. Beginning ½" from one end, glue ribbon along top edge of fringe; glue ribbon ends to wrong side of skirt.

Fig. 1

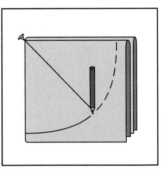

Star
1 square = 1"

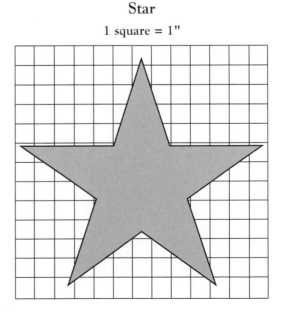

135

all that glitters (pages 38-41)

Braided Globes

You need (for each): 2½" to 4" plastic foam ball; skewer; 1 sheet of Peel n' Stick double-stick plastic; assorted braids; ¾" straight pins; glue gun; 8" of narrow ribbon; 12" of wide ribbon; tassel or acrylic-crystal drop.

Preparing globe: Insert skewer into ball. Cut Peel n' Stick into short 2"W strips; wrap and press around ball. Remove backing paper; press edges of adhesive onto ball with scraps of backing paper (do not touch adhesive with fingers).

Trimming globe: Press braid into adhesive to cover ball; place wide braid around center of ball and coil narrow braid on ends. Secure ends with pins if needed.

Finishing: Remove skewer; fill hole with glue. Tie ends of narrow ribbon together to make hanging loop; glue knot into hole. Tie wide ribbon into bow; glue to top of ball. Poke hole in bottom of ball; glue tassel cord or crystal drop into hole.

Dove Tree Topper

You need: 14" square of lightweight cardboard; heavy-duty aluminum foil; dressmaker's tracing wheel; ballpoint pen (ink cartridge removed); small pointed scissors; craft glue.

Cutting: Transfer full-size patterns onto cardboard to make dove and wing templates; cut out. Trace around templates onto foil, using tracing wheel. Using tracing wheel and pen, mark designs on each piece; refer to patterns for motifs. Using small scissors, cut out each piece about ⅛" away from outline.

Assembling: Glue lower portion of wing to front of dove; fold lower edge of wing to back of dove.

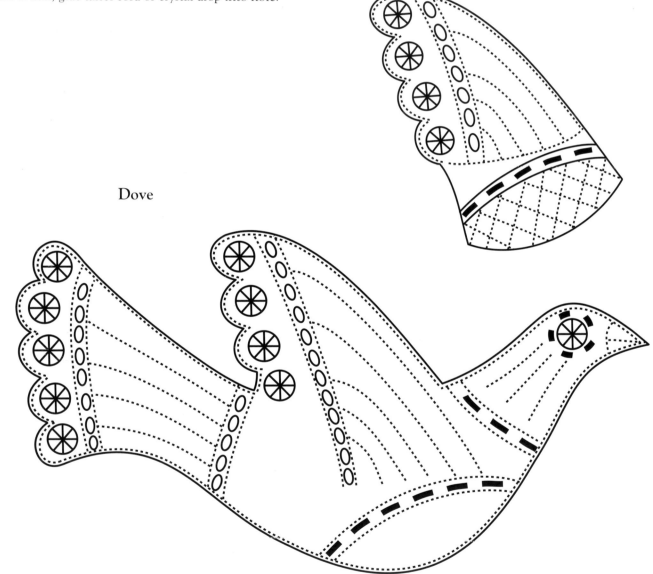

Wing

Dove

Papercut Garland

You need: 28½" x 7" piece of white paper; tagboard (manila folder); cutting mat; craft knife; craft glue; assorted silver sequins; tracing paper; dressmaker's transfer paper.

Folding the paper: Evenly fan-fold paper into 3½" wide sections.

Transferring the design: Transfer full-size pattern onto tagboard to make template; cut out. Lay template on folded paper with base of template against base of paper and straight edges of branches flush with folded edges of paper. Draw around template.

Cutting out the design: Place folded paper on cutting mat. Use craft knife to cut out the design. **Note:** *Do not cut through the edges which join the trees together.*

Finishing: Unfolded paper. Glue sequins to trees.

Tree

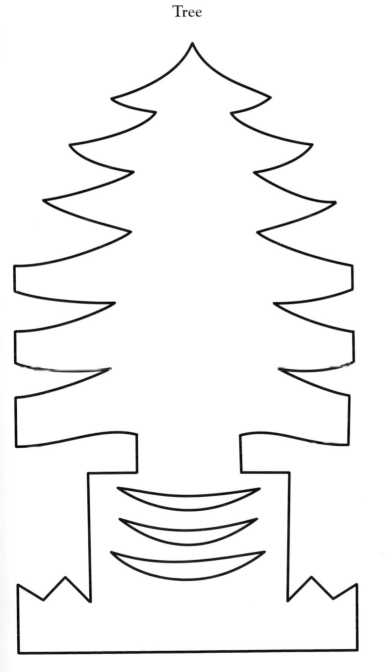

holiday style (pages 42-43)
Crocheted Snowflakes

You need: Bedspread weight cotton thread (size 10); steel crochet hook – size 6 (1.80 mm); fabric stiffener; rustproof pins; spray acrylic sealer; translucent nylon thread.

Pattern Stitch: *2-DC Cluster* – (YO, insert hook in st or sp and pull up a loop, YO and draw through 2 loops on hook) twice, YO and draw through all 3 loops on hook.

Top Snowflake: Ch 8, join with slip st to form a ring. *Rnd 1:* Ch 1, 16 sc in ring; join with slip st to first sc: 16 sc. *Rnd 2:* Ch 3 **(counts as first dc, now and throughout)**, dc in same st and in next sc, (2 dc in next sc, dc in next sc) around; join with slip st to first dc: 24 dc. *Rnd 3:* Ch 3, dc in next dc, ★ † ch 6, sc in second ch from hook and in next 4 chs, ch 4, 2-Dc Cluster in fourth ch from hook, ch 5, sc in second ch from hook and in next 3 chs, ch 7, sc in second ch from hook and in next 4 chs, ch 5, slip st in fifth ch from hook, ch 6, sc in second ch from hook and in next 4 chs, slip st in free loop of opposite ch and in next ch, ch 5, sc in second ch from hook and in next 3 chs, slip st in free loop of opposite ch and in top of 2-Dc Cluster, ch 3, slip st in ch at base of 2-Dc Cluster, ch 6, sc in second ch from hook and in next 4 chs, dc in next 2 dc, (ch 3, 2-Dc Cluster in third ch from hook) twice †, dc in next 2 dc; repeat from ★ 4 times **more**, then repeat from † to † once; join with slip st to first dc, fasten off.

Left Snowflake: *Rnd 1:* (Ch 11, slip st in 11th ch from hook) 6 times; join with slip st to first ch of first loop, fasten off: 6 loops. *Rnd 2:* Join thread with slip st in any loop; ch 1, 3 sc in same loop, ch 1, tr in next slip st, ch 1, (3 sc in next loop, ch 1, tr in next slip st, ch 1) around; join with slip st to first sc: 18 sc. *Rnd 3:* Ch 1, sc in same st and in next sc, (ch 11, slip st in 11th ch from hook) 3 times, sc in same sc and in next sc, ch 3, ★ sc in next 2 sc, (ch 11, slip st in 11th ch from hook) 3 times, sc in same sc and in next sc, ch 3; repeat from ★ around; join with slip st to first sc, fasten off.

Bottom Snowflake: Ch 6, join with slip st to form a ring. *Rnd 1:* Ch 12, slip st in fifth ch from hook, ★ † (ch 5, slip st in fifth ch from hook) twice, slip st in same ch as first slip st, ch 4, dc in ring, ch 10, slip st in second ch from hook and in next 3 chs, ch 9, slip st in second ch from hook and in next 4 chs, ch 5, slip st in third ch from hook and in next 2 chs, ch 6, slip st in second ch from hook and in next 4 chs, slip st in free loop of opposite ch and in next 3 chs, ch 5, slip st in second ch from hook and in next 3 chs, slip st in free loop of opposite ch and in next 5 chs, slip st in dc †, dc in ring, ch 9, slip st in fifth ch from hook; repeat from ★ 4 times **more**, then repeat from † to † once; join with slip st to third ch of beginning ch-12, fasten off.

Starching: Hand wash snowflake; dry flat. Soak snowflake in fabric stiffener; dry flat, holding all the pieces in place with pins. Once the snowflake is completely dry, spray with sealer. Add loop hanger using nylon thread.

Plaid Ribbon Ornaments

You need: 3" plastic foam balls; 3" red and green glass balls; red-and-green plaid ribbons in various patterns and widths (⅜" to ⅞" to 2"W); floral wire; floral tape; wire cutters; 13 mm jingle bells; glue gun.

Wrapped Glass Balls: *Version 1* – Cut two lengths of ⅞"W ribbon to go from neck to neck around ball; glue in place. Repeat with second ribbon, crossing at right angles at bottom. Glue two bows and bell at opposite sides at neck. *Version 2* – Glue a "belt" of ⅞"W ribbon around ball at center. Glue a double-loop bow and bell opposite each other on belt.

Plaid Flowers Nosegay: Use 2"W plaid ribbon. *Cutting pieces* – Use full-size patterns to cut five sets of five flower petals and one leaf. *Making center bud* – Fold a 4" length of ribbon in half lengthwise; fold both ends downward toward the center, then fold again and twist the bottom edge to hold bud shape. Wrap with floral wire to secure. OR, substitute center bud with a cluster of three jingle bells wired together to floral wire. Make a total of five center buds. *Adding petals to each center bud* – Place five petals around center bud; wrap base with floral wire. *Assembling nosegay* – Wrap base of leaf with floral wire. Place five flowers and leaf together. Twist stems together; wrap with floral tape.

Patchwork Ball: Cut leftover plaid ribbons into 1" lengths; glue onto foam ball to cover completely, overlapping edges. Glue 4" loop and jingle bells at top; glue a separate bow to top of loop.

Clothespin Snowman

You need: 3¾"H slotted wooden clothespin with round head; 1¼" wooden bead; 1" wooden bead; 1"H wooden spool; 1¼" wooden circle cutout; ¾"W wooden cutouts – 2 stars, 1 heart; acrylic paint – white, orange, red, green, black; toothpick; 6½" of black chenille stem; 4" of ⅜"W red ribbon; 8" of ⅜"W plaid ribbon; 8" of ⅛"W green ribbon; paintbrushes; small nail; hammer; glue gun.

Preparing nose: Use hammer and nail to make a small hole in center of 1" bead. Break ½" piece from toothpick.

Painting: Paint clothespin and beads white, spool and circle black, stars green, heart red, and toothpick piece orange. Paint black eyes and mouth on small bead and buttons on large bead.

Finishing: Glue toothpick piece in small hole in small bead. Glue small bead to top and clothespin in bottom opening of large bead. *Arms* – Overlap ends of chenille stem; glue overlap to back of snowman. Glue star and heart cutouts to arms. *Scarf* – Fringe ends of plaid ribbon and tie around snowman's neck. *Hat* – Glue spool to center of circle cutout; glue red ribbon around hat. *Hanger* – Glue ends of green ribbon to top of spool.

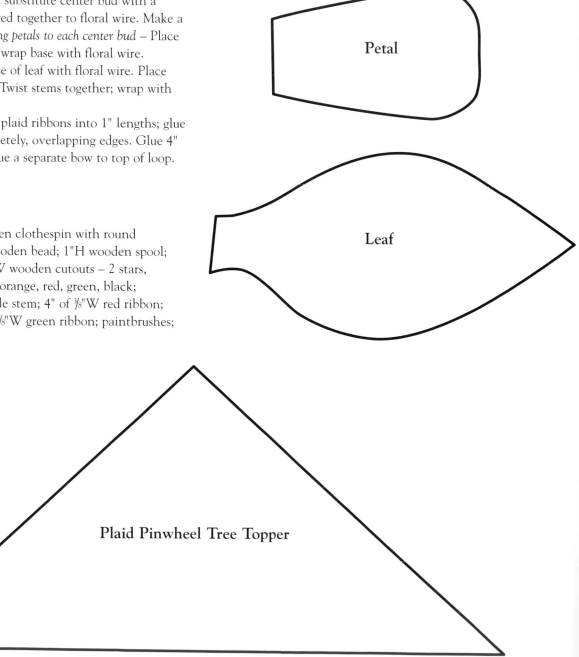

Petal

Leaf

Plaid Pinwheel Tree Topper

folksy and festive (pages 44-45)

Noel and Tree Ornaments (Continued)

Preparing appliqués: Fuse web to wrong side of appliqué fabric(s). Trace full-size pattern(s) and cut appliqué(s). Fuse appliqué(s) to background.

Embroidering: *Use six strands of floss. Noel* – Work three cross stitches for buttons and two French knots for eyes. Work straight stitches for greenery and "NOEL." *Tree* – Work straight stitches for tree.

Backing: Cut one piece of batting same size as background; cut one piece 1/8" larger on all sides. Center smaller, then larger batting pieces on wrong side of background. Use six strands of floss and work uneven blanket stitches along edges or running stitches 1/4" from edges to secure.

Adding buttons: Sew buttons to ornament as shown.

Making hanger: Cut twig to same length as top edge of ornament. Use floss to secure twig to top of ornament. Tie ends of an 8" floss length to twig ends for hanger.

Button Sweater Ornament

You need: 5" x 10" piece of felt; ten 3/8" buttons; embroidery needle; contrasting embroidery floss; 5" of narrow cord.

Cutting: Enlarge pattern; cut two sweater pieces from felt.

Sewing: Pin sweater pieces together. Stitch 1/8" seams along both sides of arms; turn.

Decorating: Sew buttons on front of sweater ornament. Using floss, embroider blanket stitches around ornament's neck, arms, and hem.

Finishing: Fold cord in half; stitch ends together to make hanging loop. Hand-stitch loop inside neck edge of ornament.

Button Sweater Ornament
Enlarge to 5" wide

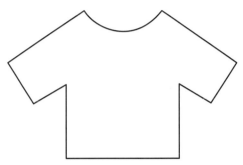

Tree Ornament

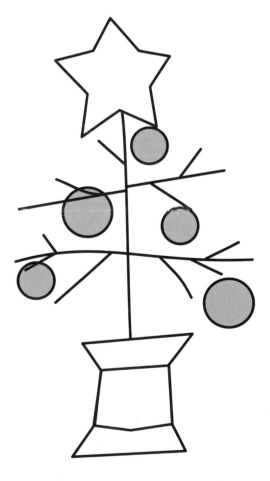

Noel Ornament

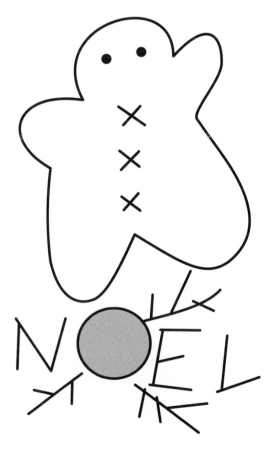

Celestial Santa Ornament

You need: 4" papier-mâché ball; acrylic paint – peach, dark pink, dark red, metallic gold, black; decorative snow paint; paintbrushes; brown waterbase stain; brown permanent felt-tip fine-point pen; ½" wooden bead; jute twine; tagboard (manila folder); drawing compass; craft knife; glue gun; paper towels.

Making circle template: Use compass to draw a 3½" circle on tagboard. Use craft knife to cut out circle; discard circle.

Drawing design: Use template to lightly draw circle on ball. Referring to *Fig. 1*, draw a crescent, approx. 1"W at widest point, in circle. Draw outline of face and hat on crescent. Draw stars on ornament as desired.

Painting: Paint hat dark red. Leaving a small triangular area unpainted for eye, paint face peach. Paint cheek dark pink. Highlight cheek using dark pink mixed with peach. Paint small black dot in unpainted area for eye. Paint stars gold. Paint rows of gold dots around stars. Use brown pen to outline stars.

Adding texture: Use a round paintbrush and a stamping motion to apply a dot of decorative snow paint for hat pom-pom. Stamp decorative snow paint over hair and beard areas. Let dry.

Antiqueing: Dip a crumpled paper towel in a very small amount of stain. Blot on a clean paper towel to remove excess. Lightly stamp decorative snow paint areas with stain.

Adding hanger: Glue ends of twine into hole of bead. Glue bead to top of ornament.

Fig. 1

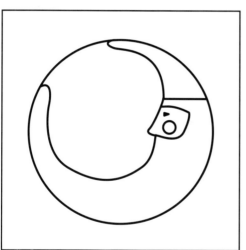

cheery checks (pages 48-51)

Pretty Poinsettia Pillow

You need: Fabrics – ½ yd blue-and-white check, ⅛ yd gold swirl print, ⅛ yd green vine print, ¼ yd red, 1 yd green-and-black check; 1⅓ yds of ⅜" cord; ¼ yd paper-backed fusible web; embroidery needle; embroidery floss – red, green, yellow; stuffing.

Cutting: Cut one 10" square background block from blue-and-white check. From gold swirl print, cut four 2¾" sashing squares. From green vine print, cut four 2¾" x 10" sashing strips.

Making appliqué: Enlarge poinsettia pattern (page 141). Trace pattern parts separately onto paper side of fusible web. Fuse patterns to wrong sides of fabrics as follows: poinsettia – red, three leaves – green vine print, two leaves – green-and-black check. Cut out pieces; fuse pieces to background block. Using narrow zigzag stitches, stitch around edges and along detail lines of poinsettia. Embroider details.

Assembling pillow top: *All stitching is done with ¼" seams, right sides facing and raw edges even, unless otherwise noted.* Pin and stitch one sashing strip to block; repeat for opposite side of block. Pin and stitch two sashing squares to ends of one sashing strip; repeat for remaining sashing strip and squares. Pin and stitch sashing strips to block.

Adding welting: Cut 3" x 48" bias strip of green-and-black check fabric, piecing as needed. Center cord on wrong side of fabric strip; fold strip over cord. Baste along strip close to cord; trim seam allowance to ½". Baste cording to right side of pillow top.

Finishing: For backing, cut a square of green-and-black check fabric same size as pillow top. Place top and backing wrong sides together. Using a ½" seam allowance, pin and stitch pieces together, leaving an opening. Turn and stuff pillow; hand sew closed.

Winter Wonderland Quilt

You need: Fabrics – *Background blocks:* ⅜ yd each blue-and-white check, green mini plaid, blue plaid (also for snowman hat), green ticking stripe, blue-and-taupe plaid, and 1¾ yds red-and-black check (also for border strips and binding); *Sashing squares, border squares, and stars:* ⅜ yd bear-and-heart gold mini print; *Sashing strips, poinsettia leaves, and backing:* 3¼ yds green vine print; *Motifs:* ⅜ yd red (for poinsettia, stocking, mitten cuff), ⅛ yd red-and-white check (for snowman, scarf, stocking), ¼ yd purple swirl print (for mittens), ¼ yd gold swirl print (for stars and tree topper), ¼ yd green check (for trees and poinsettia leaves), ⅛ yd white-on-white print (for snowman); 3 yds paper-backed fusible web; embroidery needle; embroidery floss in assorted colors; twin-size quilt batting; buttons and charms.

Cutting: For blocks, cut two 10" squares from each of the six background fabrics. From gold mini print, cut twenty 2½" sashing squares and four 4" corner squares. From green-vine print, cut thirty-one 2½" x 10" sashing strips.

Making appliqués: Enlarge patterns (pages 141-144). Trace patterns onto paper side of fusible web, spacing at least ½" apart;

trace one design for each block (except stars; use one large and one small star per block). Fuse patterns to wrong sides of fabrics. Cut out pieces along outlines. Fuse pieces to blocks. Using narrow zigzag stitches, stitch around edges of each appliqué. Embroider details.

Assembling quilt rows: *All stitching is done with ¼" seams, right sides facing and raw edges even.* Arrange blocks in four rows of three blocks each. Pin and stitch sashing strips between blocks in each row. Pin and stitch sashing strips to outer blocks in each row.

Making horizontal sashing: Pin and stitch one sashing square to sashing strip. Continue stitching, alternating squares with strips, to make row of four squares and three strips. Make four more rows in same way.

Joining blocks: Starting and ending with sashing strips, arrange strips and block rows to form center panel. Pin and stitch strips to rows to complete center panel.

Making borders: Measure length of center panel; using red-and-black check, cut two 4"W side borders to this measurement. Measure width of center panel; using red-and-black check, cut two 4"W upper/lower borders to this measurement. Pin and stitch corner square to each end of each upper/lower border. Pin and stitch side borders to sides of center panel. Pin and stitch upper/lower borders to remaining edges of center panel to make quilt top.

Assembling quilt: Cut batting and green-vine backing fabric 2" larger than top all around, piecing backing as needed. Layer backing face down, batting, and top (right side up); quilt as desired. Trim batting and backing even with top.

Binding: Cut 3"W red-and-black check fabric strips; piece strips to measure about 6 yds for binding. Fold binding in half lengthwise, wrong sides facing; press. Pin and stitch binding to edges of quilt, raw edges even. Turn binding to back of quilt; hand sew binding edges to quilt.

Poinsettia

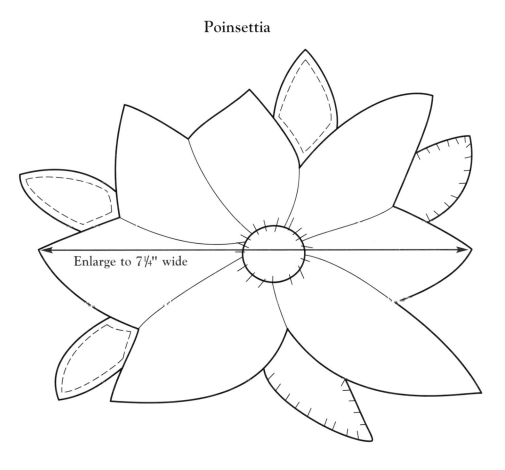

Enlarge to 7¼" wide

Snowman

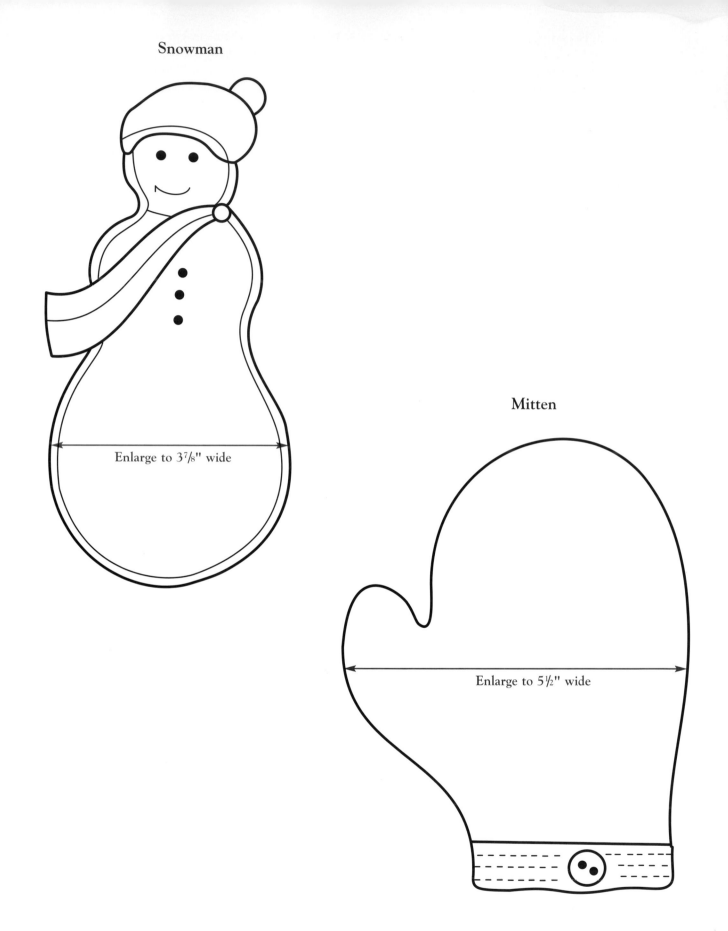

Enlarge to 3⅞" wide

Mitten

Enlarge to 5½" wide

Tree

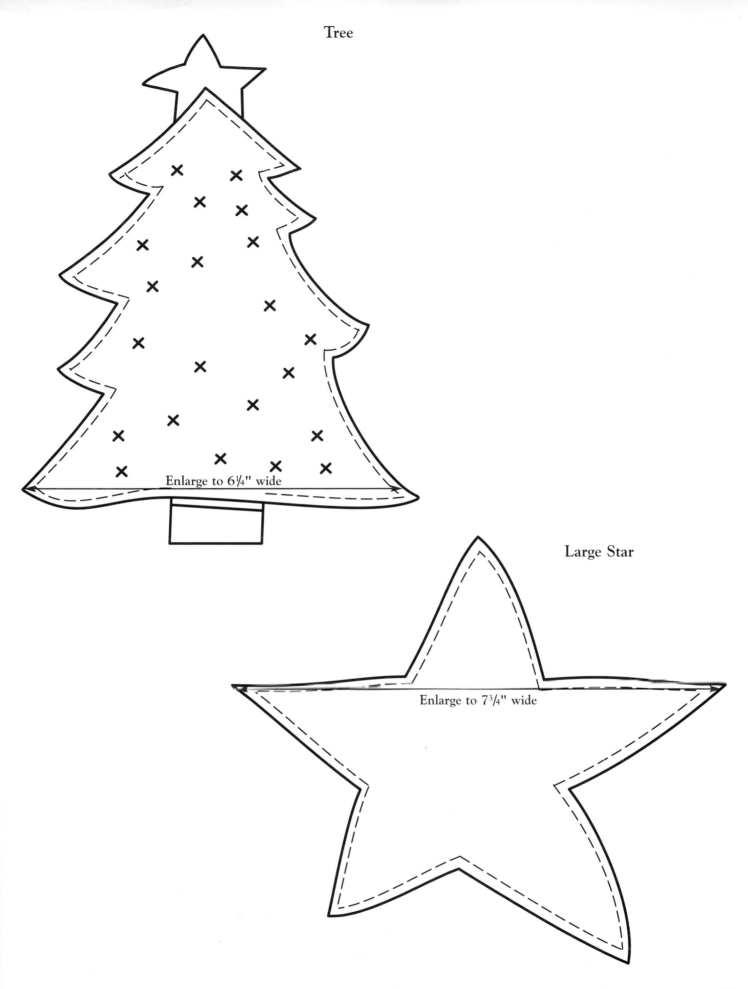

Enlarge to 6¼" wide

Large Star

Enlarge to 7¾" wide

Small Star

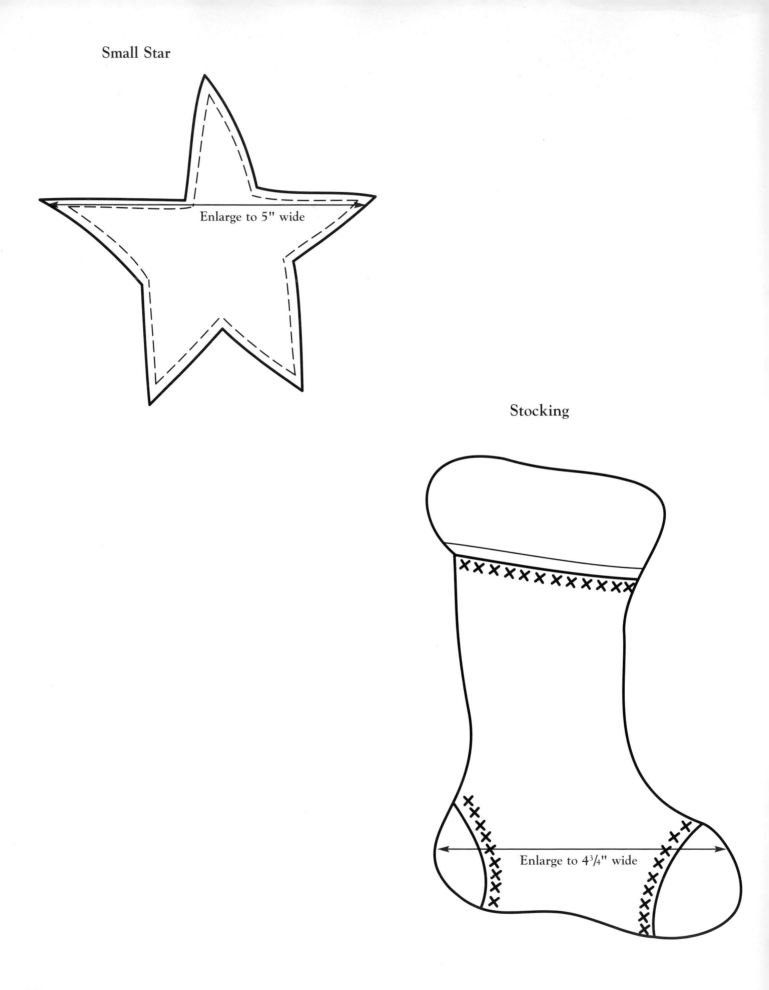

Enlarge to 5" wide

Stocking

Enlarge to 4³/4" wide

144

Cheery Checks Afghan (Continued)

To Change Colors, work last dc to within one step of completion, hook new yarn *(Fig. 1a)* and draw through both loops on hook. Carry unused yarn **loosely** across **wrong** side of work; do **not** cut yarn unless noted. When working **next** row, work **over** carried strand *(Fig. 1b)*.

Fig. 1a

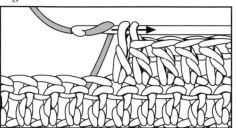

Fig. 1b

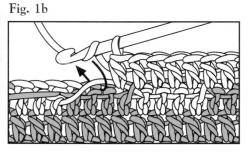

Note #2: Continue changing colors in same manner throughout.

Row 2: Ch 3 **(counts as first dc, now and throughout)**, turn; dc in next 2 dc, (with red dc in next 3 dc, with ecru dc in next 3 dc) across changing to red in last dc.

Row 3: Ch 3, turn; dc in next 2 dc, (with ecru dc in next 3 dc, with red dc in next 3 dc) across.

Row 4: Ch 3, turn; dc in next 2 dc, (with ecru dc in next 3 dc, with red dc in next 3 dc) across changing to ecru in last dc.

Row 5: Ch 3, turn; dc in next 2 dc, (with red dc in next 3 dc, with ecru dc in next 3 dc) across.

Row 6: Ch 3, turn; dc in next 2 dc, (with red dc in next 3 dc, with ecru dc in next 3 dc) across changing to red in last dc.

Rows 7-90: Repeat Rows 3-6, 21 times; at end of Row 90, do **not** change colors; cut red.

EDGING

Rnd 1: Ch 1, turn; sc in each dc across to last dc, 3 sc in last dc; 2 sc in end of each row across; working in free loops of beginning ch, 3 sc in first ch, 2 sc in next ch, sc in each ch across to marked ch, 3 sc in marked ch, 2 sc in end of each row across and in same st as first sc; join with slip st to first sc: 783 sc.

Rnd 2: Ch 1, sc in same st, ch 4, skip next 2 sc, ★ sc in next sc, ch 4, skip next 2 sc; repeat from ★ around; join with slip st to first sc, finish off.

Rnd 3: With **right** side facing, join red with slip st in any ch-4 sp; ch 4, ★ drop loop from hook, insert hook from front to back in next ch-4 sp, hook dropped loop and draw through ch-4 sp, ch 4; repeat from ★ around; join with slip st to first slip st, finish off.

Gingham Stocking Ornament

You need: 10" x 5" gingham fabric; embroidery needle; embroidery floss; pinking shears; 5" of baby rickrack; button.
Cutting: Matching short edges, fold gingham in half. Cut two 5"H stocking shapes from folded gingham. Fringe cuff edges by pulling threads for ½". Turn down 1¼" on cuff edges. Pin stocking sections together, wrong sides facing. Use floss to stitch around sides of stocking ¼" from raw edges; leave upper edge open. Pink raw edges.
Finishing: Fold rickrack in half to form hanging loop; sew ends of loop inside upper corner of stocking. Sew button at base of hanging loop.

Poinsettia Platter

You need: Clear glass platter, at least 12" across; washable marker; paintbrushes – round, fine, ¾" wash; enamel paints – green, yellow, red.
Marking designs: Draw motifs on front of platter using washable marker. Adjust spacing of checked border.
Painting: Turn platter over. Paint green and yellow dots for flower centers. Use long brushstrokes to paint red petals. Paint green leaves. Paint green line at base of rim. Paint checkerboard pattern on rim.
Finishing: Follow paint manufacturer's instructions to heat-set paint.

personal presents (pages 52-55)

Tree-and-Snowman Sweater (Continued)

Rep last 2 rows 3 times – 46 (54, 60) sts. Work even until piece measures 8 (8, 9)" from bound-off armhole sts. **Shape neck:** Work 15 (18, 20) sts, join another strand of yarn, bind off center 16 (18, 20) sts, finish row. P 1 row. Dec 1 st each neck edge on following row and work even until 9 (9, 10)" from bound-off armhole sts. Bind off rem 14 (17, 19) sts each side.

Front: Cast on and work same as back until 32 (36, 42) rows St st have been completed. *Next row* (right side): K10 (14, 17), follow chart row 1 over next 43 sts, k 9 (13, 16). Work to top of chart, at same time shaping armholes in same way as back. Continue in red until piece measures 6½ (6½, 7½)" from bound-off armhole sts. **Shape neck:** Work 16 (19, 21) sts, join another strand of yarn, bind off center 14 (16, 18) sts, finish row. P 1 row. *Next row:* K to last 4 sts on first side, k 2 tog, k2; k2, sl 1, k1, psso, finish row. P 1 row. Rep last 2 rows once. Work even until piece measures same as back to shoulders. Bind off rem 14 (17, 19) sts each side.

Sleeves: Cast on 30 sts, p 1 row. *Row 2* (right side): K2, (p2, k2) across. *Row 3:* P2, (k2, p2) across. Rep last 2 rows twice. Working in St st, inc 1 st each edge every 6th row 0 (2, 0) times, every 4th row 11 (9, 15) times – 52 (52, 60) sts. Work even until piece measures 16 (17, 18)" from beg. **Shape sleeve cap:** Work same as back-armhole shaping – 36 (36, 44) sts. P 1 row. Bind off.

Finishing: Sew one shoulder seam. **Neck:** From right side, with size-10 needles, pick up 60 (62, 64) sts evenly spaced along neck edge. P 1 row. Work 3 rows reverse St st, binding off on last row. **Nose:** With 3 strands orange yarn and size-3 needles, cast on 4 sts. Work in St st for 5 rows. *Next row:* Dec twice – 2 sts. P 1 row. K 2 tog; fasten off. Stitch to face. **Scarf:** With 3 strands blue yarn and size-3 needles, cast on 8 sts. Work in St st for 1½", ending with wrong-side row. *Next row:* Dec, k4, dec – 5 sts. Work even for 5 rows, then dec 1 at beg of row. Work even until 6"L; bind off. Cut twenty-four 3½" strands of blue yarn for fringe. Attach 3-strand fringe in each of 8 sts on first row. Stitch scarf along curve of snowman's neck. Sew ⅜" black buttons to snowman's face for eyes; sew ⅝" buttons to body. Sew remaining buttons on tree. Sew rem shoulder seam. Sew in sleeves. Sew side and sleeve seams. Embroider twig arms.

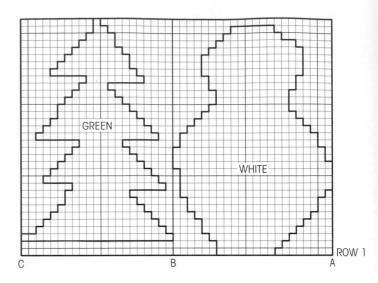

Snowman Pullover

Size: Child's sizes small (medium, large). Directions are for smallest size. Directions for larger sizes are in parentheses. If there is only one number, it applies to all sizes. Finished chest size: 32" (36", 40").

You need: Bulky weight yarn – green (600 gms, 21 oz, 720 yds), white (100 gms, 3½ oz, 120 yds); knitting needles – 1 pair each sizes 10, 9, and 3; tapestry needle; Persian yarn (8-yd skns) – 1 orange, 1 blue, 1 black; buttons – two ⅜" and three ⅝" black.

Gauge: In St st with size-10 needles, 11 sts and 14 rows = 4"; check gauge before beginning work.

Back: With size-9 needles and green yarn, cast on 48 (56, 64) sts. Beg with P row, work 3 rows reverse St st, 2 rows St st. Change to size-10 needles. *Row 6* (wrong side): P1, k2, (p2, k2) across, ending with p1. *Row 7:* K1, p2, (k2, p2) across, ending with k1. Rep last 2 rows for rib once. Continue in St st until piece measures 10 (11, 11)" from beg. **Shape armholes:** Bind off 3 sts at beg of next 2 rows – 42 (50, 58) sts. *Next Row* (dec row): K2, sl1 1, k1, psso, k to last 4 sts, k 2 tog, k2 – 40 (48, 56) sts. Work 3 rows even, rep dec row once – 38 (46, 54) sts. Work even until piece measures 7 (7, 8)" from bound-off armhole sts. **Shape neck:** Work 13 (16, 18) sts, join another strand of yarn, bind off center 12 (14, 18) sts, finish row. P 1 row. Dec 1 st each neck edge on following row and work even until 8 (8, 9)" from bound-off armhole sts. Bind off rem 12 (15, 17) sts each side.

Front: Cast on and work in same way as back until 16 (18, 18) rows St st have been completed. *Next row* (right side): K13 (17, 21), follow chart, row 1 from A to B over next 22 sts, k13 (17, 19) sts. Work to top of chart, at same time shaping armholes same as back. Continue in green until piece measures 6½ (6½, 7½)" from bound-off armhole sts. **Shape neck:** Work 14 (17, 19) sts, join another strand of yarn, bind off center 10 (12, 16) sts, finish row. P 1 row. *Next row:* K to last 4 sts on first side, k 2 tog, k2; k2, sl 1, k1, psso, finish row. P 1 row. Rep last 2 rows once. Work even until piece measures same as back to shoulders. Bind off rem 12 (15, 17) sts each side.

Sleeves: Cast on 26 sts; p 1 row. *Row 2 (right side):* K2, (p2, k2) across. *Row 3:* P2, (k2, p2) across. Rep last 2 rows once. Working in St st, inc 1 st each edge every other row 2 (0, 4) times, every 4th row 10 (12, 12) times – 50 sts. Work even until piece measures 13 (14, 15)" from beg. *Shape sleeves cap:* Work same as back-armhole shaping – 40 (40, 48) sts. P 1 row. Bind off.

Finishing: Sew one shoulder seam. **Neck:** From right side, with size-10 needles, pick up 48 sts evenly spaced along neck edge. P 1 row. Work 3 rows reverse St st, binding off on last row. **Nose, Scarf:** Same as for Tree-and-Snowman Sweater. Sew ⅜" buttons to snowman's face for eyes; sew ⅝" buttons down snowman's body. Sew rem shoulder seam. Sew in sleeves. Sew side and sleeve seams. Embroider twig arms.

Reindeer Jumper

You need: Jumper; tan fabric; 16" of ¼"W red satin ribbon; 20" of ⅝"W red grosgrain ribbon; 1 yd of ⅜"W plaid ribbon; paper-backed fusible web; covered button hardware for five ⅞" buttons; ¼" red shank button with shank removed; tan embroidery floss; fabric paint – white, black; paintbrushes; black permanent felt-tip pen with fine point; fabric glue; glue gun.

Making fence: Cut two 7½" lengths from satin ribbon and six 3" lengths from grosgrain ribbon; trim each 3" length to a point at one end. Arrange ribbons on jumper (see photo). Use fabric glue to secure.

Painting reindeer: Cover buttons with tan fabric. Draw face pattern on buttons. Paint eyes white with black pupils. Paint nose black. Highlight nose and pupils with white. Use black pen to draw mouth.

Making ears: Cut two pieces of tan fabric. Fuse fabric pieces wrong sides together. Use ears pattern and cut out five ears. Tie floss tightly around center of each ears.

Finishing: Hot glue ears to top back of reindeer. Hot glue red button to one reindeer over nose. Cut five 7" lengths from plaid ribbon; tie into bows. Sew bows and reindeers to jumper. Use four strands of floss and long stitches to stitch antlers.

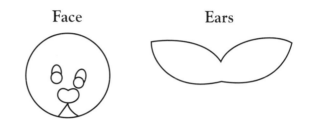

Face   Ears

Festive Ties

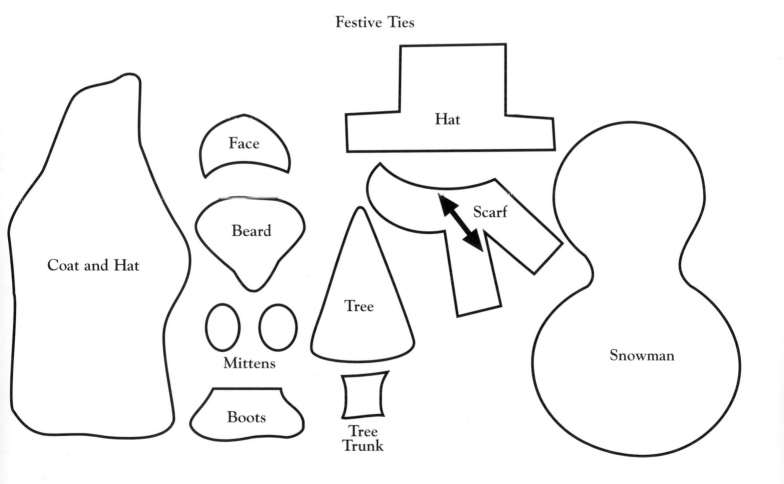

Hat

Coat and Hat

Face

Beard

Mittens

Boots

Tree

Tree Trunk

Scarf

Snowman

Cozy Fleece Slippers

You need: Polar fleece – 8" x 17" plaid, ¼ yd gold; 8" x 17" quilt batting; ¼ yd faux leather; yellow embroidery floss; needle.

Cutting fabric: Enlarge patterns. Cut two toes from plaid fleece, two toes and two soles from gold fleece (lining). Cut two soles each from batting and leather.

Stitching: *Toe* – Pin curved edges of plaid toe together; stitch dart. Repeat for lining. Pin plaid and lining pieces together, right sides facing; stitch, leaving opening at side. Turn; stitch closed. *Sole* – Pin leather and lining together, right sides facing, with batting on top; stitch, leaving opening. Turn; stitch closed.

Finishing: With floss, embroider edge of toe with blanket stitches. Pin toe to sole, linings facing; hand-sew.

1 square = 1"

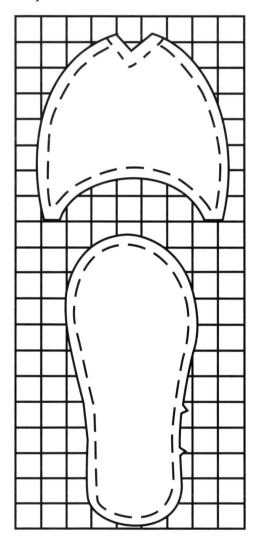

Great Gloves

You need (for each pair): Knit gloves; 10-count waste canvas – two 2" squares; lightweight non-fusible interfacing; embroidery floss (see key); needle.

Preparing gloves: Baste waste canvas to each glove; baste interfacing to inside of glove under canvas.

Stitching design: Stitch desired design on each glove using four strands of floss for cross stitches and three for French knot.

Finishing: Dampen canvas slightly to remove sizing. Use tweezers to pull out canvas threads. Trim interfacing close to design.

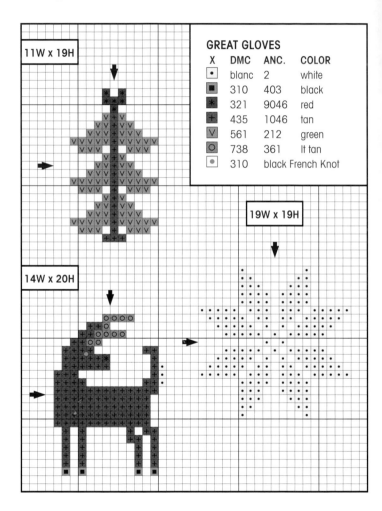

GREAT GLOVES			
X	DMC	ANC.	COLOR
•	blanc	2	white
■	310	403	black
*	321	9046	red
+	435	1046	tan
V	561	212	green
O	738	361	lt tan
•	310		black French Knot

Gift-Wrap Romper (Continued)

Arrange streamer as shown, bunching it up slightly to create ripples; pin at intervals to romper. Stitch across ribbon at end and across ribbon in three or four places in between, but avoid stitching into the wired edges.

Painting: Slide a piece of cardboard inside romper to protect back of romper from bleed-through paint. Apply paint in squiggly lines, extending from behind bow. Paint dots around ribbing on neckband and on sleeve and ankle cuffs.

Poinsettia and Holly Jacket

You need: Dry-cleanable wool jacket; red wool felt; tapestry yarn – dark yellow, red, green, dark green, brown; red embroidery floss; brush-off stabilizer; dry-cleanable paper-backed fusible web; permanent felt-tip pen.

Preparing: Dry-clean jacket, felt, yarn, and floss to prevent dyes from fading onto jacket.

Embroidering holly: Use pen to trace each full-size color holly pattern onto stabilizer. Baste patterns to jacket following **Fig. 1**. Follow stitch key and use one strand of yarn to work holly design over stabilizer. Follow manufacturer's instructions to remove stabilizer.

Appliquéing poinsettia: Fuse web to one side of felt. Use full-size patterns A - D to cut petals from felt. Referring to **Fig. 2**, arrange petals on jacket; fuse. Use two strands of red floss to work blanket stitches along edges of petals. Use one strand of dark yellow yarn to work French knots in center of poinsettia.

Fig. 1   **Fig. 2**

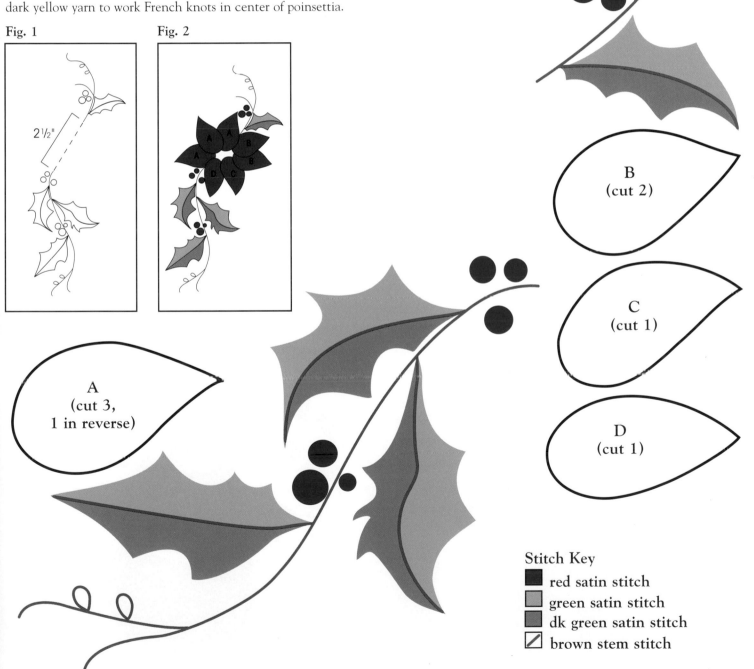

2½"

A
(cut 3,
1 in reverse)

B
(cut 2)

C
(cut 1)

D
(cut 1)

Stitch Key
- red satin stitch
- green satin stitch
- dk green satin stitch
- / brown stem stitch

149

Lollipop Lapel Pin

You need: Size 10 cotton crochet thread – small amount white, small amount red; steel crochet hook – size 5 (1.90 mm); stuffing; cotton swab; ¾" bar pin; 6" of ⅛"W ribbon; craft glue.

Front: *Rnd 1 (Right side):* With white, ch 4, 11 dc in fourth ch from hook; join with slip st to top of beginning ch – 12 sts. (*Note:* Mark last round as *right* side.) *Rnd 2:* Ch 3 changing to red in last ch, dc in same st changing to white, ★ dc in next dc changing to red, dc in same st changing to white; repeat from ★ around; join with slip st to top of beginning ch-3, finish off – 24 sts.

Back: *Rnd 1 (Right side):* With white, ch 4, 11 dc in fourth ch from hook; join with slip st to top of beginning ch – 12 sts.

(*Note:* Mark last round as *right* side.) *Rnd 2:* Ch 3 changing to red in last ch, dc in same st changing to white, ★ dc in next dc changing to red, dc in same st changing to white; repeat from ★ around; join with slip st to top of beginning ch-3 changing to red, do not finish off – 24 sts.

Joining: Holding Front and Back *wrong* sides together, with Back facing, and working through *inside* loops of *both* pieces, slip st in each st around to last st, stuffing lightly before closing, leave last st unworked; finish off.

Finishing: Cut off one end of cotton swab; insert opposite end into lollipop between unworked stitches; glue. Glue pin to back. Add ribbon bow.

finishing touches (pages 56-57)

Stencil Motifs
Enlarge to desired size

150

last-minute gifts (pages 58-59)

Snowman Towel

You need: Cotton dish towel; fabric paint – white, black, orange; paintbrushes; dressmaker's transfer paper; black permanent felt-tip pen.

Preparing towel: Wash, dry, and press towel.

Painting: Use full-size pattern and transfer paper to transfer design to towel. Paint snowman body white. Use black paint to add buttons, mouth, eyes, and hat to snowman. Use orange paint to paint nose. Outline snowman nose and body with pen.

Wood Frames

You need: Unfinished wood frames; acrylic paint – red, green; paintbrushes; sandpaper.

To do: *Red frame* – Paint frame green; dry. Paint red; dry. Sand to reveal green paint. *Green frame* – Paint frame red; dry. Paint green; dry. Sand same as above for red frame.

Glitzy Napkins

You need (for each): Cloth napkin; gold metallic fabric paint; paintbrush.

Preparing napkin: Wash, dry, and press napkin.

Painting: Paint napkin as desired, using full-size patterns if needed.

Snowman

Circle

Star

Crocheted Teddy Bear (Continued)

Dec A, ★ 1 sc in each of next 3 sts, Dec A, 1 sc in each of next 2 sts, Dec A, rep from ★ once, 1 sc in each of next 3 sts, Dec A – 19 sc. *Row 41:* Ch 1, Dec A, (1 sc in next st, Dec A) twice, 1 sc in each of next 3 sts, (Dec A, 1 sc in next st) twice, Dec A – 13 sc. *Row 43:* Ch 1, Dec A, (Dec B) 3 times, Dec A – 5 sc. *Row 44:* Rep Row 2; fasten off.

Head – Front Piece: Ch 20. *Row 1* (right side): Sk 1 ch, 1 sc in each ch to end – 19 sc. *Row 2 and alt rows:* Ch 1, Loop st in each sc to end. *Row 3:* Ch 1, 2 sc in 1st st, (1 sc in each of next 5 sts, 2 sc in next st) twice, 1 sc in each of next 5 sts, 2 sc in last st – 24 sc. *Row 5:* Ch 1, 2 sc in 1st st, 1 sc in each of next 7 sts, 2 sc in next st, 1 sc in each of next 2 sts, 2 sc in each of next 2 sts, 1 sc in each of next 2 sts, 2 sc in next st, 1 sc in each of next 7 sts, 2 sc in last st – 30 sc. *Row 7:* Ch 1, 2 sc in 1st st, 1 sc in each of next 9 sts, 2 sc in next st, 1 sc in each of next 3 sts, 2 sc in each of next 2 sts, 1 sc in each of next 3 sts, 2 sc in next st, 1 sc in each of next 9 sts, 2 sc in last st – 36 sc. *Row 9:* Ch 1, 2 sc in 1st st, 1 sc in each st to last st, 2 sc in last st – 38 sc. *Row 11:* Rep Row 9 – 40 sc. *Row 13:* Ch 1, sc in each of first 9 sts, Dec A, 1 sc in each of next 6 sts, Dec A, 1 sc in each of next 2 sts, Dec A, 1 sc in each of next 6 sts, Dec A, 1 sc in each of next 9 sts – 36 sc. *Row 15:* Ch 1, 1 sc in each of 1st 9 sts, Dec A, 1 sc in each of next 4 sts, Dec A, 1 sc in each of next 2 sts, Dec A, 1 sc in each of next 4 sts, Dec A, 1 sc in each of next 9 sts – 32 sc. *Row 17:* Ch 1, 1 sc in each of 1st 9 sts, Dec A, (1 sc in each of next 2 sts, Dec A) 3 times, 1 sc in each of next 9 sts – 28 sc. *Row 19:* Ch 1, 1 sc in each of 1st 10 sts, Dec A, 1 sc in each of next 4 sts, Dec A, 1 sc in each of next 10 sts – 26 sc. *Row 21:* Ch 1, 1 sc in each st to end. *Row 23:* Ch 1, Dec A, 1 sc in each of next 4 sts, Dec A, (1 sc in each of next 2 sts, Dec A) 3 times, 1 sc in each of next 4 sts, Dec A – 20 sc. *Row 25:* Ch 1, Dec A, ★1 sc in each of next 2 sts, Dec A, 1 sc in next st, Dec A, rep from ★ once, 1 sc in each of next 2 sts, Dec A – 14 sc. *Row 27:* Ch 1, (Dec A) 3 times, 1 sc in each of next 2 sts, (Dec A) 3 times – 8 sc. *Row 29:* Ch 1, Dec A, (1 sc in next st, Dec A) twice – 5 sc. *Row 30:* Rep Row 2; fasten off.

Back Piece: Ch 20. *Row 1* (right side): Sk 1 ch, 1 sc in each ch to end – 19 sc. *Row 2 and alt rows:* Ch 1, Loop st in each sc to end. *Row 3:* Ch 1, 2 sc in 1st st, 1 sc in each of next 6 sts, 2 sc in next st, 1 sc in each of next 3 sts, 2 sc in next st, 1 sc in each of next 6 sts, 2 sc in last st – 23 sc. *Row 5:* Ch 1, 2 sc in 1st st, 1 sc in each st to last st, 2 sc in last st – 25 sc. *Row 7:* Ch 1, 2 sc in 1st st, 1 sc in each of next 8 sts, 2 sc in next st, 1 sc in each of next 5 sts, 2 sc in next st, 1 sc in each of next 8 sts, 2 sc in last st – 29 sc. *Row 9:* Ch 1, 2 sc in 1st st, 1 sc in each st to last st, 2 sc in last st – 31 sc. *Row 11:* Ch 1, 2 sc in 1st st, 1 sc in each of next 10 sts, 2 sc in next st, 1 sc in each of next 7 sts, 2 sc in next st, 1 sc in each of next 10 sts, 2 sc in last st —35 sc. *Row 12:* Rep Row 2. *Row 13:* Ch 1, 1 sc in each st to end. Rep

Rows 12 and 13 three times, then Row 12 once. *Row 21:* Ch 1, Dec A, 1 sc in each of next 6 sts, Dec A, 1 sc in each of next 3 sts, Dec A, 1 sc in each of next 5 sts, Dec A, 1 sc in each of next 3 sts, Dec A, 1 sc in each of next 6 sts, Dec A – 29 sc. *Row 22 and alt rows:* Rep Row 2. *Row 23:* Ch 1, Dec A, 1 sc in each of next 4 sts, Dec A, 1 sc in each of next 2 sts, Dec A, 1 sc in each of next 5 sts, Dec A, 1 sc in each of next 2 sts, Dec A, 1 sc in each of next 4 sts, Dec A – 23 sc. *Row 25:* Ch 1, Dec A, 1 sc in each of next 2 sts, Dec A, 1 sc in next st, Dec A, 1 sc in each of next 5 sts, Dec A, 1 sc in next st, Dec A, 1 sc in each of next 2 sts, Dec A – 17 sc. *Row 27:* Ch 1, (Dec A) 3 times, 1 sc in each of next 5 sts, (Dec A) 3 times – 11 sc. *Row 29:* Ch 1, Dec B, Dec A, 1 sc in next st, Dec A, Dec B – 5 sc. *Row 30:* Rep Row 2; fasten off.

Ears: Outer piece: Ch 11. *Row 1* (right side): Sk 1 ch, 1 sc in each ch to end – 10 sc. *Row 2 and alt rows:* Ch 1, Loop st in each sc to end. *Row 3:* Ch 1, 1 sc in each st to end. *Row 5:* Rep Row 3. *Row 7:* (Dec A) 5 times – 5 sc. *Row 8:* Rep Row 2; fasten off.

Inner piece: Work same as Outer Piece, working in sc only.

Legs: Ch 30. *Row 1* (right side): Sk 1 ch, 1 sc in each ch to end – 29 sc. *Row 2:* Ch 1, Loop st in each sc to end. *Row 3:* Ch 1, 1 sc in each st to end. Rep Rows 2 and 3 twice, then Row 2 once. **Foot Shaping:** *Row 9:* Ch 1, 1 sc in each of 1st 13 sts, Dec B, 1 sc in each of next 13 sts – 27 sc. *Row 10 and alt rows:* Rep Row 2. *Row 11:* Ch 1, 1 sc in each of 1st 12 sts, Dec B, 1 sc in each of next 12 sts – 25 sc. *Row 13:* Ch 1, 1 sc in each of 1st 11 sts, Dec B, 1 sc in each of next 11 sts – 23 sc. *Row 15:* Ch 1, 1 sc in each of 1st 10 sts, Dec B, 1 sc in each of next 10 sts – 21 sc. Rep Rows 2 and 3 eight times, then Row 2 once; fasten off. **Foot Pads:** Ch 7. *Rnd 1:* Sk 1 ch, 3 sc in next ch, 1 sc in each of next 4 ch, 3 sc in last ch, working along other side of foundation ch, 1 sc in each of next 4 ch, sl st in 1st sc – 14 sc. *Rnd 2:* Ch 1, 2 sc in same place as sl st, 2 sc in each of next 2 sc, 1 sc in each of next 4 sc, 2 sc in each of next 3 sc, 1 sc in each of next 4 sc, sl st in last sc – 20 sc. *Rnd 3:* Ch 1, 1 sc in same place as sl st, 1 sc in next sc, 2 sc in each of next 2 sc, 1 sc in each of next 8 sc, 2 sc in each of next 2 sc, 1 sc in each of next 6 sc, sl st in last sc – 24 sc. *Rnd 4:* Ch 1, 1 sc in same place as sl st, 1 sc in each of next 2 sc, 2 sc in each of next 2 sc, 1 sc in each of next 10 sc, 2 sc in each of next 2 sc, 1 sc in each of next 7 sc, sl st in last sc – 28 sc; fasten off.

Left Arm: Ch 23. *Row 1* (right side): Sk 1 ch, 1 sc in each ch to end – 22 sc. *Row 2:* Ch 1, Loop st in each sc to end. *Row 3:* Ch 1, 1 sc in each st to end. Rep Rows 2 and 3 nine times. *Row 22:* Ch 1, Loop st in each of 1st 13 sc, 1 sc in each of next 9 sc. *Row 23:* Rep Row 3. Rep Rows 22 and 23 twice. *Row 28:* Ch 1, Loop st in each of 1st 13 sc, Dec A, 1 sc in each of next 5 sc, Dec A – 20 sc. *Row 29:* Ch 1, Dec A, (1 sc in each of next 3 sts, Dec A) twice, (1 sc in each of next 2 sts, Dec A) twice – 15 sc. *Row 30:* Ch 1, Loop st in each of next 10 sc, 1 sc in each of next 5 sc; fasten off.

Right arm: Work to correspond to left arm.
Assembling: Do not press. Attach eyes and nose to head. Join seams of body, head, and arms; stuff each part. Sew foot pads to legs, then join leg seams and stuff. Sew head, arms, and legs to body. Sew ear pieces together in pairs and sew in position, leaving 3" between ears. If desired, cut loops open. Tie ribbon bow around neck.

Teddy Bear Wreath

You need: 20" artificial evergreen wreath; 3 teddy bears (approx. 6"-8" tall) dressed in sweaters, scarves, and hats; miniature snow shovels, ice skates, and sled; assorted size white pom-poms; artificial snow; wire-edge ribbon; craft glue; floral wire; glue gun.
Making snowballs: Apply craft glue to pom-poms; roll in artificial snow.
Bears: Use floral wire to attach bears to wreath. Hot glue one shovel, ice skates, and sled to bears' paws.
Finishing: Hot glue remaining snowballs and shovel to wreath. Tie ribbon into a multi-loop bow and wire to wreath. Sprinkle artificial snow over wreath.

creations for kids (pages 62-63)

Home Sweet Home

You need: Cardboard; masking tape; 3 large egg whites; electric mixer; 16 ounces confectioners' sugar; pastry bag with #4 tip; assorted candies.
Assembling: Use full-size pattern and cut one front section, one back section, two 6" x 4¾" sides, and two 7¼" x 5" roof sections from cardboard. Assemble pieces; tape edges together.
Decorating: With electric mixer, beat together egg whites and confectioners' sugar on high speed until fluffy and thick, about 5 minutes; spoon into pastry bag. Pipe icing onto one area of cottage at a time; cover with candies.

Front and Back

Create-A-Cookie Kit

You need: White Chocolate Cookie Dough and Edible "Paints" (recipes below); cookie cutters; painter's drop cloth; large paintbrushes; new, small paintbrushes; metal pail; white gesso; green acrylic paint; glossy clear acrylic spray sealer.

Painting pail: Use large paintbrush to apply two coats of gesso to entire pail. Paint inside of pail green; paint outside of pail with green to resemble dripping paint. Spray pail with sealer.

Assembling kit: Place drop cloth, dough, "paints," cookie cutters, and small paintbrushes in pail. Give with instructions for making cookies. **Note:** *Dough and "paints" should not be left unrefrigerated for more than 30 minutes. Instruct kit recipient to keep food items refrigerated until ready to bake.*

White Chocolate Cookies

Cookie Dough:

- 5 cups all-purpose flour
- 1 teaspoon baking soda
- 1 teaspoon salt
- 1 cup butter or margarine, at room temperature
- 1½ cups sugar
- 2 eggs
- 1 teaspoon vanilla
- 2 packages (6 ounces each) white baking chocolate, melted

Edible "Paints":

- 3 egg yolks
- Green, red, and blue liquid food coloring

1. Cookie Dough: In large bowl, sift together flour, baking soda, and salt. In another large bowl, beat butter and sugar until light and fluffy. Beat in eggs and vanilla until well blended; beat in melted chocolate.

2. Stir dry ingredients into creamed mixture. Knead until a soft dough forms, sprinkling with water, if necessary, to hold dough together. Place dough in a resealable plastic bag and store in refrigerator.

3. Edible "Paints": Drop each yolk into a separate small bowl. Stir each yolk with a fork until smooth. For green, add ¼ teaspoon green food coloring to one bowl; mix well. For red, add ½ teaspoon red food coloring to second bowl; mix well. For black, add 1¼ teaspoons green, 1½ teaspoons red, and five drops blue food coloring to third bowl; mix well. Place each color "paint" in a small jar with lid and store in refrigerator. Give with instructions below for making cookies.

4. To make cookies: Let dough come to room temperature. Preheat oven to 350°. Roll out dough onto floured surface to ¼-inch thickness. Cut out cookies using cookie cutters. Place ½ inch apart on greased baking sheets. Repeat, rerolling scraps.

5. Use paintbrushes and "paints" to decorate cookies.

6. Bake in preheated 350° oven for 7 to 10 minutes or until bottoms are lightly browned. Remove cookies from baking sheets to wire racks to cool.

Yield: Makes about 5 dozen 3½-inch-high cookies

Christmas Candy

You need: Worsted weight yarn (see key); one 10⅞" x 13⅞" sheet of 7 mesh plastic canvas; #16 tapestry needle; 4"L lollipop stick; white sewing thread; clear cellophane; craft glue.

Making Tree Nougat Candy (2¼"W x 2¼"H): Cut and stitch Tree Nougat Front/Back and Side, leaving shaded areas unworked. To join ends of Side, match ✱'s and work stitches in shaded areas through both thicknesses. Use red to join Front and Back to Side. Wrap an 8" square of cellophane around Candy. Use thread to tie cellophane in place.

Making Lollipop (2⅞"W x 7½"H): Cut and stitch Lollipop Front/Back. Glue a lollipop stick to wrong side of Back between ▲'s. Matching ▲'s, use candy color to join Front to Back along unworked edges. Wrap an 8" square of cellophane around Candy. Use thread to tie cellophane in place.

Making Peppermint (2¼"W x 6½"H): Cut and stitch Peppermint Front/Back and Side, leaving shaded areas unworked. To join ends of Side, match ✱'s and work stitches in shaded areas through both thicknesses. Use color to match stitching area to join Front and Back to Side. Wrap an 8" square of cellophane around Candy. Use thread to tie cellophane in place.

Making Ribbon Candy (1½"W x 1½"H): Cut and stitch Ribbon Candy piece, leaving shaded areas unworked. Turn piece over and work stitches in shaded areas. Thread needle with an 18" length of candy color yarn. Refer to *Fig. 1* to bend piece. (**Note:** When piece is properly positioned, only the right side of stitching will show.) Starting at one end of folded piece, insert needle through all thicknesses at ◆'s. With same yarn, insert needle back through all thicknesses at ●'s. Pull yarn until Candy is approximately 1½"H. Knot yarn close to Candy.

Fig. 1

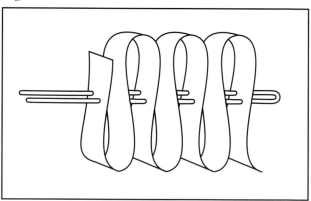

Lollipop Front/Back (19x19 threads) (Work 2)

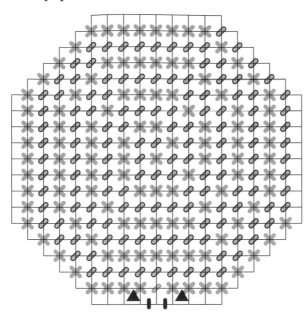

Tree Nougat Front/Back (15x15 threads) (Work 2)

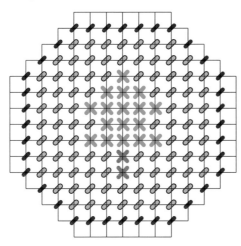

Peppermint Front/Back (15x15 threads) (Work 2)

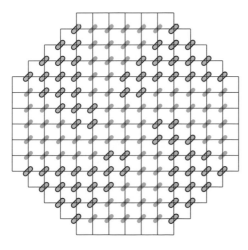

	white
	red
	green
	brown
	candy color

Tree Nougat Side
(3x49 threads)

Peppermint Side
(3x49 threads)

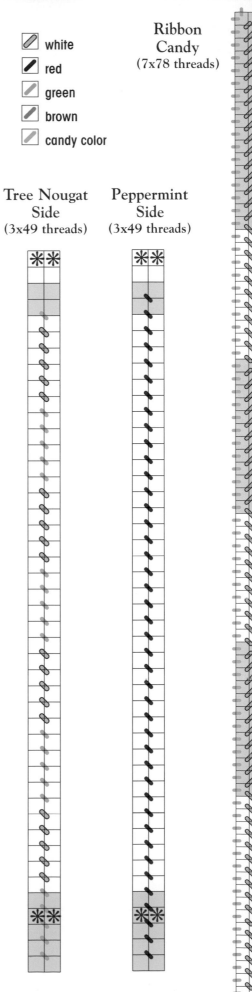

Ribbon Candy
(7x78 threads)

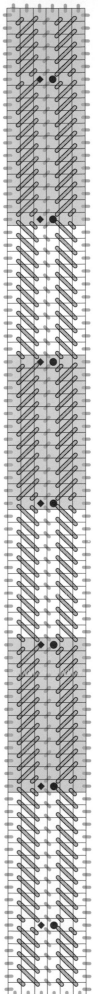

155

let it glow (pages 76-77)

Scented Candles

These instructions are for making scented candles from scratch. However, you can use the same embellishing techniques to decorate purchased candles.

You need (for each candle): Premium candle wax (about 2 lbs per candle); double boiler; candle or candy thermometer; packages of concentrated candle dye and scent; package of metal-core wick with screw (size depends on mold diameter); metal mold in desired shape; thin dowel or pencil; mold sealer; pouring container with spout; skewer; candle-gloss spray.

Melting wax: Break wax into small pieces; place in upper pot of double boiler. Fill lower pot with water; place on stove. Place thermometer in wax; heat to 190°F, stirring constantly. Add dye and scent, following manufacturer's suggested amounts. **Note:** *Never leave melting wax unattended.*

Preparing mold: Thread wick through bottom hole in mold. Place dowel across top of mold; tie end of wick to dowel. Turn mold over; cut wick to 1". Wind wick around screw head; secure bottom with mold sealer. Heat mold by running warm water over outside of mold.

Pouring candle: Pour wax into pouring container. Tilt mold; slowly pour in wax to desired candle height. Reserve about one cup wax to fill indentation, which will form in center of candle as it sets. Let candle set for one hour. Poke skewer into candle on side of wick to remove pressure, which builds up as candle sets. Reheat reserved wax; pour into indentation (do not pour wax higher than height of previous pour).

Finishing: Let candle set overnight. Remove mold sealer and screw; untie knot. Turn mold upside down so candle slips out.

Embellishing: Use low-melt hot glue gun to attach cinnamon sticks, dried fruit slices, or dried flowers to candle. Melt additional wax; quickly dip embellished candle to seal. Let set. To attach cloves, trim stems to $\frac{1}{8}$". Heat tip of awl; poke hole in candle. Insert clove into hole before wax sets. Coat with candle-gloss spray.

stockings to hang

(pages 78-79)

Jester Stockings (Continued)

Clip curves; do not turn. Stitch cuff sections together along jagged edges; trim seam allowances and clip into corners. Stitch side seams of cuff. Fold cuff, right sides out and raw edges even. Stitch cuff to upper edge of stocking. Fold hanging loop in half lengthwise, right sides facing. Stitch long edge; turn. Fold loop in half. Stitch loop to upper corner of stocking, raw edges even. Stitch upper edge of lining to upper edge of stocking, over loop. Turn right side out; turn lining to inside of stocking. Fold cuff to outside.

Finishing: Hand-stitch bells to points of cuff.

Felt Stockings

You need (for all three): 44"/45"W felt – $\frac{1}{3}$ yd each red, blue, green, $\frac{1}{8}$ yd gold; embroidery floss – red, blue, yellow, green; embroidery needle.

Cutting: *For each* – Enlarge patterns. Cut two stockings (front and back), one cuff, one $\frac{3}{4}$" x 7" strip for loop. Cut hearts and stars (see photo).

Hearts/stars: Pin motifs to one (front) stocking piece. With full strand of floss, stitch shapes in place with running stitches.

Assembling: *Stocking* – Pin front and back pieces together, right sides out. With full strand of floss, stitch together with running stitches, $\frac{1}{4}$" from edges; leave top open. *Cuff* – Run a row of running stitches $\frac{1}{4}$" from sawtooth edge. Lap cuff ends to form ring; stitch overlap. Turn stocking. Pin right side of cuff to wrong side of stocking. *Loop* – Run a row of running stitches on each side. Fold strip in half; slip between stocking and cuff. Machine-stitch around cuff/stocking; turn.

Felt Stockings

Small	1 square = $\frac{5}{8}$"
Medium	1 square = $\frac{3}{4}$"
Large	1 square = 1"

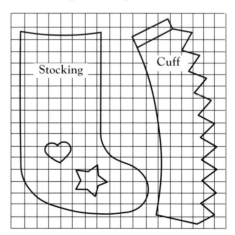

Jester Stockings

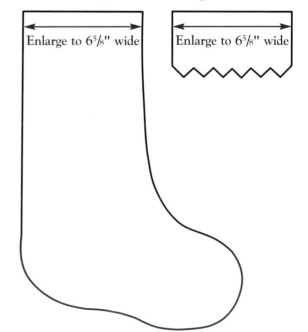

Enlarge to $6\frac{5}{8}$" wide

basic how-to's

How to Enlarge Patterns

We recommend making enlargements on a copier – it's fast and accurate. Use the "enlarge" button; repeat copying and enlarging until you get the desired size. For some patterns (such as Jolly Santa Doll, page 113), you may also use the grid method: Copy the pattern one square at a time onto 1"grid graph paper to get a full-size pattern.

Cross Stitch

Cross Stitch

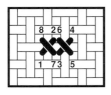

¼ Cross Stitch

½ Cross Stitch

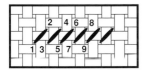

Backstitch

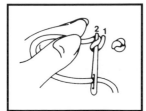

French Knot

Embroidery

Blanket Stitch

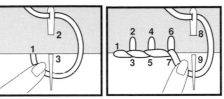

Overcast Stitch

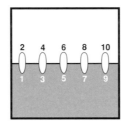

Running Stitch

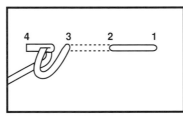

Satin Stitch

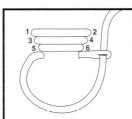

Straight Stitch

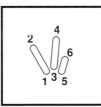

Stem Stitch

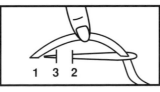

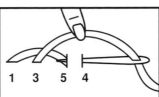

Needlepoint and Plastic Canvas Needlepoint

Tent Stitch

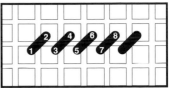

Gobelin Stitch

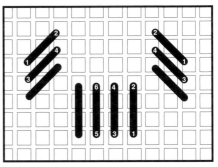

Cross Stitch

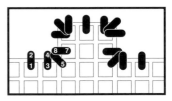

Overcast Stitch

Crochet and Knit Abbreviations

beg – beginning	**Rnd** – Round
ch(s) – chain(s)	**sc** – single crochet
ch-1 – chain-1	**sk** – skip
dc – double crochet	**skns** – skeins
dec – decrease	**sl** – slip
inc – increase	**sp(s)** – space(s)
k – knit	**St st** – Stockinette
lp – loop	stitch
mm – millimeters	**st** – stitch
P – purl	**tog** – together
psso – pass slipped	**tr** – treble crochet
stitch over	**yds** – yards
rem – remaining	**YO** – yarn over
rep – repeat	

how-to's index

recipe index

credits

To Magna IV Color Imaging of Little Rock, Arkansas, we say thank you for the superb color reproduction and excellent pre-press preparation.

To the talented people who helped create the following projects and recipes in this book, we extend a special word of thanks:

- Karin Bagan: #1 on pg. 46.
- Joanne Beretta: *Jolly Santa Doll,* pg. 14.
- Amy Albert Bloom: *Saint Nick Letter Box,* pg. 15.
- Bea Cihak: *Nut Crescents, Apricot Wraps, Double-Mint Drops, Anise Pine-Nut Drops,* pg. 88; *Piña Colada Drops, Peanut Butter and Jelly Shortbread, Butterscotch-Pecan Slices,* pg. 89.
- Jill Fanuzzi: *Felt Ornaments,* pg. 35.
- Adrianne Franklin: *Winter Wonderland Quilt,* pg. 49.
- Kathleen George: *Braided Globes,* pg. 41.
- Stephanie Gildersleeve: *Tree-and-Snowman Sweater, Snowman Pullover,* pg. 52.
- Leslie Hemmings: *Jester Stockings,* pg. 78.
- Lauren Hunter: *3-D Gingermen Ornaments,* pg. 23.
- Julio Jimenez: *Berry and Bay Wreath,* pg. 74.
- Kathy Lamancusa: *Pinecone Star,* pg. 21.
- Amy Leonard: #2 on pg. 46; #4 on pg. 46; *Gingham Stocking Ornament,* pg. 51; *Wood Frames,* pg. 59; #1 on pg. 80; #5 on pg. 81.
- Karin Lidbeck: *Star-Struck Sneakers,* pg. 54.
- Lina Morielli: *Ginger Skater,* pg. 23.
- Patricia Nese: *Personalized Bushel Basket,* pgs. 34 and 35.
- Off the Beaten Path: *Scented Ginger Garland,* pg. 23.
- Allison Pew: *Button Sweater Ornament,* pg. 45.
- Regina Ragone: star cookies, pgs. 34 and 35.
- Sheila Haynes Rauen: *Poinsettia Platter,* pg. 51.
- Eileen Raymond: *Glimmer Stars,* pg. 41.
- Nancy Roth: *Frosty Family,* pg. 24.
- Deborah Schneebeli-Morrell: *Dove Tree Topper,* pg. 39; *Papercut Garland,* pg. 41 (from **Easy & Elegant Christmas Crafts by Deborah Schneebeli-Morrell.** Copyright © 1997 by Deborah Schneebeli-Morrell. Reprinted by permission of Facts on File, Inc.).
- Mimi Shimmin: *Felt Stockings,* pg. 79.
- Karen Tack: *Home Sweet Home,* pg. 62; #3 on pg. 30.
- Douglas Turshen and Rochelle Udell: *Sparkling Topiary Tower,* pg. 40.
- Jim Williams: *Star Tree Topper,* pg. 36.
- Lois Winston: *Christmas Sampler,* pg. 29.
- Lesly Zamor of Bloom: *Fragrant Fancy Wreath, Jolly Holly Wreath,* pg. 75.

Special acknowledgment is given to the following *Family Circle* photographers:

- Antonis Achilleos: bottom right, pg. 7; bottom, pg. 24; right, pg. 31; top right, pg. 47; bottom, pg. 51; pgs. 62, 68-71, 87-89.
- Nicholas Baratta: top left, pg. 47; pg. 52.
- John Bessler: top right, pg. 7; pgs. 18-19; right and bottom left, pg. 23; bottom left, pg. 29; top right, pg. 46; center, pg. 72; top right pg. 73; top right, pg. 77; pg. 78.
- Monica Buck: bottom left, pg. 45; top, pg. 51; pg. 74.
- Steve Cohen: center and left, pg. 46; bottom right, pg. 47; pgs. 56-57; bottom left, pg. 59.
- Gary Denys: top right, pg. 54; top left, pg. 55.
- Tria Giovan: bottom left, pg. 7; pg. 8; top and bottom right, pg. 9; center left, pg. 73.

- Brian Hagiwara: pg. 66.
- Bill Holt: pg. 15; top right, pg. 33.
- Kit Latham: pgs. 20, 79.
- Kevin Lein: pg. 36.
- Taylor Lewis: top, pg. 76.
- ©Libelle: top and bottom, pg. 6; top, pg. 30.
- Michael Luppino: center left, pg. 7; pg. 21; bottom right, pg. 30; pgs. 38-41, 49; center, pg. 80.
- Joshua McHugh: bottom left, pg. 54.
- Jeff McNamara: left, pg. 9; bottom, pg. 22; #6 on pg. 31; pgs. 34-35; top left, pg. 73; top left, pg. 81.
- Steven Mark Needham: pgs. 67, 82.
- Dean Powell: bottom right, pg. 46; bottom left, pg. 47; top, pg. 80; middle left, pg. 81.
- Alan Richardson: pg. 14; pg. 32; bottom left, pg. 33; top left, pg. 59; pg. 60; bottom right, pg. 72; pg. 75; top left and bottom left, pg. 77; pgs. 84-86; pgs. 90-105.
- Steve Tague: top right, pg. 81.
- Steve Wisbauer: pg. 13.

We also wish to thank the following *Family Circle* photography stylists:

- Betty Alfenito: pgs. 69, 70, 92, 94.
- Denise Canter: pgs. 90, 93; bottom, pg. 96.
- Cathy Cook: pg. 74.
- Kim Freeman: #6 on pg. 7; pg. 8; top and bottom right, pg. 9; center left, pg. 73.
- Petra Henttonen: pg. 82.
- Edward Kemper Design: pgs. 68, 71, 95; top, pg. 96; pgs. 97, 99.
- Christine McCabe: pg. 66.
- Matthew Mead: bottom left, pg. 45; pg. 74.

Thanks also go to the following *Family Circle* food stylists:

- Baked Ideas: right, pg. 31; bottom right, pg. 7.
- A. J. Battifarano: pg. 91; top, pg. 96; pgs. 100-105.
- Roscoe Betsill: pg. 97.
- Cathy Cook: pgs. 69, 70, 84-88, 91, 100-105.
- Kevin Crafts: pg. 95.
- Anne Disrude: pgs. 92, 94.
- Rick Ellis: pg. 93.
- William Smith: top and bottom, pg. 71; pg. 90; bottom, pg. 96; pg. 99.
- Andrea B. Swenson: bottom left, pg. 33; pgs. 66-67.
- Karen Tack: pg. 68; center, pg. 71; pgs. 84-89.

The set for *Jolly Santa Doll,* pg. 14 was constructed by Bill the Set Builder; hairstyles for models on pg. 52 by Mateo for Bumble & Bumble; makeup for models on pg. 52 by Jennifer Martin.

Food consulting was provided by JoAnn Brett for *Chocolate-Orange Cookies,* pg. 91, and *Peppermint Cream Puffs,* pg. 92; by The Family Circle Food Department for *Spiced Pear Butter,* pg. 67; and by Paul E. Piccuito for *Jalapeño Honey Mustard with Sun-Dried Tomatoes, Cranberry-Ginger Vinegar, Bourbon-Spiked Butterscotch Sauce,* pg. 67, and *Marinated Skewered Shrimp, Tapenade Toasts, Mushroom and Brie Tartlets, Butternut-Leek Bisque, Caesar Salad with Crispy Croutons, Peppered Rib Roast, Thyme Roasted Potatoes, Green Beans with Roasted Hazelnuts, Fennel and Red Pepper Gratin,* pgs. 100-104.

We want to especially thank Leisure Arts photographers David Hale, Jr., Mark Mathews, Larry Pennington, Karen Shirey, and Ken West of Peerless Photography and Jerry R. Davis of Jerry Davis Photography, all of Little Rock, Arkansas, for their time, patience, and excellent work.